Wissenschaftliche Beiträge aus dem Tectum Verlag

Reihe Wirtschaftswissenschaften

Wissenschaftliche Beiträge
aus dem Tectum Verlag

Reihe Wirtschaftswissenschaften
Band 98

Marina Lipski

CSR in the German Mittelstand

Development and Implementation

Tectum Verlag

Die Deutsche Nationalbibliothek verzeichnet diese Publikation
in der Deutschen Nationalbibliografie; detaillierte bibliografische Daten
sind im Internet über http://dnb.d-nb.de abrufbar.
The Deutsche Nationalbibliothek lists this publication in the Deutsche Nationalbibliografie;
detailed bibliographic data are available on the Internet at http://dnb.d-nb.de
ISBN 978-3-8288-4614-2 (Print)
978-3-8288-7683-5 (ePDF)
978-3-8288-7684-2 (ePub)

British Library Cataloguing-in-Publication Data
A catalogue record for this book is available from the British Library.
ISBN 978-3-8288-4614-2 (Print)
978-3-8288-7683-5 (ePDF)
978-3-8288-7684-2 (ePub)

Library of Congress Cataloging-in-Publication Data
Marina Lipski
CSR in the German Mittelstand
Development and Implementation
Wissenschaftliche Beiträge aus dem Tectum Verlag;
Reihe Wirtschaftswissenschaften, Bd. 98
116 pp.
Includes bibliographic references.
ISBN 978-3-8288-4614-2 (Print)
978-3-8288-7683-5 (ePDF)
978-3-8288-7684-2 (ePub)

Umschlaggestaltung: Tectum Verlag, unter Verwendung des Bildes # 1408585988
von Wright Studio | www.shutterstock.com

1. Auflage 2021

Gesamtverantwortung für Druck und Herstellung
bei der Nomos Verlagsgesellschaft mbH & Co. KG.

Gedruckt auf alterungsbeständigem Papier.

Table of Contents

List of Tables

List of Figures

List of Abbreviations

BDI .... Bundesverband der Deutschen Industrie e.V.

CSR .... Corporate Social Responsibility

EC .... European Commission

EY .... Ernst & Young GmbH

GmbH .... Gesellschaft mit beschränkter Haftung (limited company)

GRI .... Global Reporting Initiative

IfM Bonn .... Institut für Mittelstandsforschung Bonn (Research Center of German Mittelstand in Bonn)

MNE .... Multinational Enterprise

OECD .... Organisation for Economic Cooperation and Development

PC .... Percentage Change

SME .... small and medium-sized enterprise

TRM .... Total Responsibility Management

UN .... United Nations

UNESCO .... United Nations Educational, Scientific and Cultural Organization

Acknowledgements

I wish to express my sincere appreciation to my university supervisor, Dr Olga Kuznetsova, whose expertise was invaluable when writing my Master's thesis and this book. Her insightful and honest feedback pushed me to sharpen my thinking and brought my work to a higher level.

Also, I would like to acknowledge my partner, Yuri Popov, for his constant support and willingness to help. I really appreciate our intense discussions that were a constant source of inspiration.

Foreword

When nearly two decades ago I was interviewing a senior manager of one of the UK utility companies, a conversation had drifted into discussing the desirability, practicality and feasibility of having a designated CSR managerial role in organisations. A preferable scenario my interviewee wanted to see enacted was for such a role to become ubiquitous, reflecting the understanding that social and societal responsibilities were not any more a peripheral concern for for-profit businesses.

Nowadays this view is far more common than even could be hoped for back in the day, in a great measure because of persistent research in social responsibility that helped the practitioners to recognise CSR as a strategic element of corporate performance. At the same time, thanks to CSR scholarship, it has become apparent that the complexity of the societal issues that corporate social activities are expected to address require substantial resources and expertise, putting a strain even on the biggest of business operations.

Despite the proliferation of the 'value for society' mentality and culture, even well-managed companies do not always seem to prefer a total integration of CSR into their business strategies. Instead, activities focusing on delivering value for society are often spearheaded by a variety of managers via a range of not always perfectly coordinated programmes.

While big companies can afford to have a portfolio of programmes, coordinated or dispersed, small and medium-sized organisations have no choice but to be more discerning when selecting targets for their societal impact and integrating appropriate relevant actions into their operations. In this respect, the analysis of the engagement with CSR of the firms of German *Mittelstand*, proposed in this study, offers a timely opportunity to develop practical recommendations for strategizing CSR implementation in small and medium firms.

To be effective when responding to societal commitments, businesses unavoidably find it essential to learn what it takes to align their initiatives not just with the societal expectations but also with the institutional contexts. The value of this book in this respect is that it offers insights into the working of small and medium-sized enterprises in the context of a co-ordinated market economy, of which Germany is a prime example.

The publication of *CSR in the German Mittelstand* is especially welcome in the current circumstances as small and medium enterprises are bracing themselves to face the challenges of the post-COVID-19 reconstruction that inevitably will force them to review the priorities and affordability of the choices they make.

28 January 2021

Dr Olga Kuznetsova

Reader in Comparative Business Studies

Manchester Metropolitan University, UK.

Abstract

Increasingly aware of the advantages and rewards of corporate social responsibility (CSR), more small and medium-sized companies (SMEs) are interested in engaging in CSR. This book focuses on the German Mittelstand, which consists mostly of SMEs and is considered a role model for other economies. Despite the demand for appropriate CSR implementation, research concerning the CSR-SME relationship is still underdeveloped and requires more generalisable results. The following determinants of CSR engagement were synthesised into a conceptual framework: awareness, motivation/goals, challenges, activities, and communication. This book examines the development of CSR engagement in the German Mittelstand and outlines trends that will allow better recommendations for CSR implementation. Unlike many investigations of CSR in the SME context, which rely on a qualitative methodology, this book utilised large-scale secondary data from four surveys from the years 2007, 2012, and 2017 to conduct a quantitative analysis with the statistical method index numbers and percentage change. This approach provides conclusions about the changes in drivers and barriers in CSR engagement, also considering different size classes of SMEs.

The results indicate a positive trend toward the issue, including increased topic importance and frequency of CSR activities, decreased challenging factors, and intensified communication. Overall, a strong, economically orientated CSR approach of the Mittelstand-firms is observable. The comparison of the firms' size classes revealed minor differences in CSR engagement, suggesting SMEs' alignment with the CSR engagement of large enterprises is only a matter of time. Therefore, a structured and organised CSR approach is required. This approach should consider the results of this work, which provide important trends for the key factors of CSR implementation.

1. Introduction

Since the 1960s, the idea of corporate social responsibility (CSR), relating to a company's responsibility to society and a broad range of stakeholders, has become increasingly important (Wang et al., 2016). The European Commission (EC) (2011:6) defines CSR as 'the responsibility of enterprises for their impacts on society' and emphasises that firms need to consider CSR. Due to the economic and financial crisis and especially the G8 summit in 2007, calls for more responsibility in business have grown. During this time, the German Ministry of Labour and Social Affairs within the federal government took the lead on the topic of CSR. The Ministry founded the National CSR Forum as a body in which a variety of social actors work together on 'corporate responsibility'. Based on its recommendations, the German Federal Government adopted the CSR Action Plan in 2010, which was implemented in the following years, further spreading CSR in Germany (Bundesministerium für Arbeit und Soziales, 2020).

The focus on CSR is still on large companies and corporations (Kechiche and Soparnot, 2012). However, due to the considerable number of small and medium-sized companies (SMEs) that profoundly affect the environment, economy, and society, this sector started to receive more attention within the CSR movement (Spence, 1999; Spence et al., 2003; Jenkins, 2004; Jenkins, 2006). Furthermore, SMEs differ from large companies in terms of size and ownership, which must be considered for the implementation of CSR (EC, 2015; Kechiche and Soparnot, 2012). Thus, SMEs do not only have a massive impact on the economy and the environment but demonstrate that CSR is also significantly important for smaller companies (Spence et al., 2003; Jenkins, 2004). In addition, authors like Jenkins (2004) and Carroll and Brown (2018) confirm that CSR applies to smaller companies, despite the term 'corporate'.

In this context, the work focuses on German Mittelstand-companies. The 'Mittelstand' is a terminological peculiarity in German-speaking countries, and these firms are defined by the unity of ownership and management. A company's qualitative characteristics, rather than its size, is the deciding factor for a company belonging to the Mittelstand. These characteristics are the following: the significant influence of the owner on management issues, the bearing of entrepreneurial risk by the owner, and the securing of the livelihood of the owner/management (IfM Bonn, 2020a). Nearly all German Mittelstand-companies are

SMEs, but the Mittelstand also includes a small part of larger firms that exceed the criteria for SMEs. Moreover, family enterprises and owner-managed firms are equivalent to Mittelstand-firms. To clarify the difference between Mittelstand-firms and SMEs, the Research Center of German Mittelstand in Bonn (IfM Bonn) (2020b) established quantitative criteria, maximum 500 employees and a maximum of EUR 50 million of annual revenue, categorising an enterprise as an SME. Even if a firm exceeds the quantitative criteria of an SME, according to the IfM Bonn (2020b), it can be still a Mittelstand-company if it meets the qualitative criteria outlined previously. In this book, Mittelstand-companies and SMEs are treated as synonyms because the largest part of the Mittelstand are SMEs, thus making the relevant literature in the CSR-SME relationship applicable to the Mittelstand.

Since the 1990s, interest in the CSR-SME relationship has increased, and theoretical and empirical research has been conducted (Spence, 1999; Maldonado-Erazo et al., 2020). Carroll's CSR pyramid, the stakeholder theory, social capital, and other models have contributed to the theoretical foundation of this investigation field. For this work, the synthesis of these models, theories, schools of thought, and empirical evidence led to identification of the key factors of CSR engagement: awareness, motivation/goals, activities, challenges, and communication. Many authors (EC, 2015; Maldonado-Erazo et al., 2020) argue that the literature concerning CSR in SMEs is still underdeveloped; therefore, academic research is required, especially in the German context. Although some research has been completed, it is mainly limited to qualitative methods and small samples, preventing generalisations (Maldonado-Erazo et al., 2020). Therefore, an analysis of the development considering determining factors of CSR engagement in German Mittelstand-companies would be highly beneficial. This analysis would provide an understanding of the essential aspects for these firms, drivers of CSR engagement, the origin of difficulties, and potentials the Mittelstand-firms could use. Thus far, no research has investigated the development of CSR engagement in the German Mittelstand. Mittelstand-firms and institutions supporting German firms can especially profit from this research's findings. While the German Mittelstand is internationally considered a role model for other economies (IfM Bonn, 2020c), this study's findings can also benefit companies in other regions by considering the development and trends of CSR engagement. The book adopts a quantitative approach, analysing data from between 2007 to 2017 and using secondary data from the Bertelsmann Stiftung (2007),

Gilde *Gesellschaft mit beschränkter Haftung* (GmbH) (2007), Ernst & Young GmbH (EY) (2012), and Pott et al. (2017).

Therefore, the book examines the development from the start of increased interest for CSR in Germany in 2007 until the newest available empirical data in 2017. This ten-year period allows for conclusions about the emerging long-term changes and trends. The work focusses especially on the determination of the development of CSR engagement concerning the key factors awareness, motivation/goals, activities, challenges, and communication; the development of the key factors to the firms' different size categories; and the main changes and the trend of CSR engagement in these firms.

This book begins by providing a literature review presenting the main terminology and language in the CSR-SME relationship. This chapter also includes a discussion about the knowledge accumulated so far concerning CSR in SME business environment. Further, important theories, models, and empirical evidence are presented and synthesised into a conceptual framework underpinning the work. The third chapter is concerned with the research design used for this book. Chapter 4 presents the results of the quantitative analysis. The fifth chapter discusses the results of the analysis, focusing on the key factors of CSR engagement. Chapter 6 presents managerial implications and practical approaches for the CSR implementation. The last chapter summarises the main findings, provides recommendations, and outlines the limitations.

2. Literature Review

2.1 The Applicability of CSR in SMEs

Jenkins (2004) argues that researchers often do not clearly define 'corporate' or 'corporation', supposing that the notion of a large enterprise is understood and accepted. Fuller and Tian (2006) state that much of the academic literature on CSR is directed toward large companies, and other authors (Williamson et al., 2006; Fassin et al., 2011) argue that multinational enterprises (MNEs) take a leading role in the CSR agenda. However, the exclusive focus on MNEs' social engagement neglects the significant role of SMEs entirely (Jenkins, 2004). The Research Institute of the German Mittelstand in Bonn (IfM Bonn, 2020d) emphasises that 99.5% of all enterprises are SMEs in Germany, so there were 3.5 million SMEs with around 17 million employees in 2018. These enterprises employed 58% of the workforce in private business that generated 35% of the overall turnover in Germany (IfM Bonn, 2020d). Jamali et al. (2009) state that the realisation of the massive impact of SMEs led to rising interest of international organisations and governments to incentivize SMEs' engagement in CSR.

In contrast to the vague definition of 'corporate', Jenkins (2004) argues that the investigation of SMEs is always connected to explicit definitions isolating SMEs from corporations as a different class of businesses. Furthermore, Roberts et al. (2006) stress that within the CSR investigation area, the outlined linguistical problem leads to the alienation of SMEs. Jenkins (2004:52) continues his argumentation, stating that 'SMEs are frequently seen as a problem within the CSR debate, because of their failure to become engaged with it. An alternative interpretation is that it is the CSR debate that is the problem, because of its failure to engage SMEs'. Besser and Miller (2001) address this issue by replacing the term 'corporate' with 'business', emphasising that the inclusion of all kinds of business is thereby ensured and can no longer be the determining factor of social responsibility trends. Additionally, Castka et al. (2004) explain that the word 'corporate' should be regarded on a larger scale, enabling the inclusion of all businesses independent of their size, structure, industry, and ownership. Furthermore, Murillo and Lozano (2006) propose the term 'responsible competition', and Lepoutre and Heene (2006) suggest 'small company social responsibility'. However, Preuss and Perschke (2010) argue that all businesses, not just large firms, are in charge of society and a new term like 'business social responsibility', stressing the entirety of firms, would not be a useful contribution to the academic discussion. Instead, Preuss and Perschke (2010) underline that the application of CSR in the SME context does not lead to a loss of clarity. Jenkins (2004:40) points out that isolation of SMEs in the CSR context is not valid and concludes that 'there is no reason to suppose that most discussions of CSR do not apply to SMEs'. Carroll and Brown (2018) confirm that despite the usage of the term 'corporate', CSR refers to all forms of businesses, including small, medium, and large companies.

Several authors (Russo and Perrini, 2010; Murillo and Lozano, 2006), continuing the terminological discussion, claim the definition of CSR is counterproductive and inoperative for SMEs because of the strong orientation toward larger firms in the establishment of standards. Over the years, many CSR definitions have been suggested, but no uniform definition exists (McWilliams et al., 2006). Vázquez-Carrasco and López-Pérez (2013) criticise that nearly all definitions refer to stakeholders, like the CSR definition of the EC (2011:6):

> To fully meet their corporate social responsibility, enterprises should have in place a process to integrate social, environmental, ethical, human rights and consumer concerns into their business operations and core strategy in close collaboration with their stakeholders, with the aim of: maximising the creation of shared value for their owners/shareholders and for their other stakeholders.

Lynch-Wood et al. (2009) and Jenkins (2006) explain that the stakeholder focus is not adequate because this term is not common in many SMEs. Moreover, Russo and Perrini (2010) claim that CSR can be applied to different concepts in SMEs. Perrini (2006) states that SMEs often engage in CSR but do not use this specific term to address their activities or they are unaware of their CSR activities. Here, Gilde GmbH (2007) provides empirical evidence from German SMEs showing that these firms' actions have a social, economic, and environmental influence, but the term CSR is not customary.

In addition, Vázquez-Carrasco and López-Pérez (2013) argue that the essence of CSR lies in the adoption of socially responsible business practices, business cultures, and appropriate attitudes rather than the formalisation of the concept, its processes, or the discussion of terminology addressing the same issue. Furthermore, Vázquez-Carrasco and López-Pérez (2013) address CSR reporting widely applied in large companies using a more formal and technical language. The absence of CSR reporting or the application of a more accessible language in SMEs does not mean that these firms are not acting socially responsibly. The authors claim that a specific focus in the SME business context and adoption of the informal nature of these firms' business styles is required for CSR (Vázquez-Carrasco and López-Pérez, 2013).

Jamali et al. (2009) deliberate that the discord in terminology concerning the focus of CSR on large corporations leads to the question of whether there are differences in the CSR approach for SMEs and large businesses. This issue is discussed in the next section.

2.2 Development of CSR in the SME Context

As Vázquez-Carrasco and López-Pérez (2013) identified, CSR is increasingly important for large companies as well as for SMEs. However, Maldonado-Erazo et al. (2020) claim that the intensity of integration of CSR in SMEs is far less than in the corporate context, although CSR within SMEs has been an established study field since the 1990s. Vázquez-Carrasco and López-Pérez (2013), who summarised the CSR in SME research, concluded that SMEs understand their social responsibility, and thus, there is demand for more CSR studies and research into small business realities. Moreover, Russo and Tencati (2009) recommend the creation of guidelines, aiming to support growth opportunities and promote socially responsible positioning.

Vázquez-Carrasco and López-Pérez (2013:3216) found that the analysis of the academic contribution of CSR in SMEs is a 'very relevant line of research with a lot of potential for future studies'. This finding also confirms the current publication by Maldonado-Erazo et al. (2020:15), stressing that 'this topic does not reach maturity, due to the limited presence of quantitative and confirmatory studies, a situation completely contrary to that of more general CSR research in corporate contexts'.

The profile of SMEs has significant differences from larger enterprises regarding their structural, functional, or social aspects (Perrini et al., 2007; Jenkins, 2006; Davies and Crane 2010). According to Preuss and Perschke (2010), it is essential that SMEs have a high degree of heterogeneity, making the generalisation of results difficult. Many authors, for instance, Jenkins (2004), Russo and Tencati (2009), and Preuss and Perschke (2010), emphasise that SMEs are not smaller versions of large firms, and Maldonado-Erazo et al. (2020:4) add that the 'CSR concept has had to adapt to SMEs'. As many authors (Morsing and Perrini, 2009; Von Weltzien and Shankar, 2011) found, the SME sector can make a massive contribution to society, and Murillo and Lozano (2006) recommend the investigation of this type of business. Moreover, Spence and Rutherfoord (2003) explain that smaller enterprises are the dominant method of business organisation. Morsing and Perrini (2009:2) reasoned, due to the endeavours of practitioners, scholars, and politicians to understand and promote CSR engagement, that 'an improved understanding of current CSR practices in SMEs has the potential of stimulating a high impact for the global economy and society as well as for the SMEs themselves'.

When evaluating the organisation of SMEs, SMEs are often owner-managed companies where the owner's decisions have a dominant role in business operations and significantly influence the CSR approach. Furthermore, SMEs tend to employ a personalised style of management and lack formal management structures with specialised employees (Jenkins, 2006). In comparison, Bos-Brouwers (2010) explain that large corporations have delegated management control between shareholders and the board of directors. They often respond to a range of stakeholders and emphasise the importance of shareholders.

In contrast, Jenkins (2004) and Lepoutre and Heene (2006) describe smaller businesses' responsibility as mostly limited to few stakeholders and their impact on the regional or local community instead of the wider extent of society. Here, Fuller and Tian (2006) emphasise that the more 'human' management is based in the owner-managed leadership style, leading to a greater likelihood of integrity and honesty. Jamali et al. (2009) argue that such behaviour is the result of a value-driven, philanthropic approach, including personal satisfaction. However, this statement seems to be a contradiction of one of SMEs' greatest goals, that is, as Jenkins (2006) state, the company's economic survival instead of maximising profits. Vázquez-Carrasco and López-Pérez (2013) stress that this management style is compatible with a pragmatic approach from SME management and positive economic outcomes. Thus, Fassin (2008) indicate that SMEs aim to implement a long-term perspective to minimise the risk of failure.

However, everyday operational pressure consists of several short-term tasks that must be solved concurrently. The dominant position of the entrepreneur can lead to intuitive decisions and ad hoc processes that support the assumption of informality and reduced professionalism (Spence and Rutherfoord, 2001; Fisher et al., 2009; Spence, 1999). Large companies are highly formalised and incorporate clear demarcation, planning, control measures, and defined strategies that cause organisational costs. Hence, SMEs are characterised by flat and flexible management structures, allowing them to react quickly and potentially adapt to changing circumstances (Jenkins, 2006).

According to Davies and Crane (2010), the integration of CSR into SMEs boosts employee satisfaction. Furthermore, integration strengthens loyalty, and Hamman et al. (2009) outline that CSR implementation leads to reduced costs, increased efficiency, increased attraction and retainment of qualified employees, and improved relationships with local communities.

Jenkins (2004) observed that SMEs focus on risk avoidance, thus paying attention predominantly to financial and operational risks and considering other risk types depending on the individual situation and the manager's business approach. Additionally, many SMEs have a lack of resources that hinder the deliberation of activities not directly related to the enterprise. These issues are apparent in accessing financial resources, time, and skilled staff (Kechiche and Soparnot, 2012).

Morsing and Perrini (2009) found that, due to the SMEs' size, they are more likely to be affected by pressure from business customers along the supply chain. This issue can result in the danger of dependency and the necessity to adopt specific CSR standards to maintain relationships with large business partners (Jenkins, 2004). In contrast to large businesses, SMEs have fewer expenditures to protect their reputations and, therefore, must mainly protect and strengthen their customer business due to their lack of beneficial marketing strategies (Jenkins, 2004). Hence, Spence et al. (2003) reason that smaller businesses are strongly attached to their region and focus on meeting customer needs with local knowledge and connectedness.

To date, existing studies demonstrate the importance of CSR in the SME context and simultaneously highlight the lack of scholarly work on this topic. The literature concerning German firms indicates that the majority of German SMEs engage somehow in CSR (Maaß and Clemens, 2002; Gilde GmbH, 2007; Maaß, 2007, 2010; Maaß et al., 2014; Abel-Koch, 2017; Pott et al., 2017). A recent study found that 66% of the German population had great trust in SMEs. In contrast, only 31% expected appropriate social, environmental, and economic responsibility from large companies or corporations (Buschhausen, 2016). A company's need to implement a CSR strategy arises from trends such as demographic and climate change (Kranzusch et al., 2017). Consequently, the pressure of publicity as well as a firm's needs, lead to the necessity of an appropriate CSR approach for SMEs in Germany.

Although many German companies conduct CSR activities in their business operations, the implementation of a structured and extensive CSR approach for SMEs has not yet been realized (Abel-Koch, 2017; Pott et al., 2017). However, the implementation of CSR into a business strategy requires more awareness and understanding of potential benefits grounded in the assumption that profit growth and CSR are not conflicting aims for SMEs in Germany (Maaß, 2007). These observations indicate a need to analyse the current development of CSR engagement in German SMEs and outline trends that will allow for better recommendations for CSR implementation.

2.3 Key Factors of CSR Engagement in SMEs

As discussed, the importance of CSR in SMEs and the awareness of this topic in academic literature has increased in in recent years. Here, determining the drivers' and barriers' impact on CSR engagement in SMEs is of interest. Carroll (1979:500) defined CSR as 'the economic, legal, ethical, and discretionary expectations that society has of organizations at a point in time' and later concretised 'discretionary' as 'philanthropic' due to its real manifestation in business practice (Carroll, 1991). Today, Carroll's pyramid model is widely recognised in CSR research.

Referring to Carroll's CSR pyramid (1991), Jamali et al. (2009) argue that SMEs may prioritise and pay attention to some types of responsibility more than to others. Further, Von Weltzien and Shankar (2011) claim that CSR should be seen in SMEs as a value-building factor regardless of whether the motivation is altruistic. According to Jenkins (2006), motivation to implement CSR differs depending on the business case. Over the last few decades, the following theories have been developed to explain companies' reasons for and methods of CSR engagement, for example, stakeholder theory, resource-based view, agency theory, and social capital (Mellahi et al., 2016; McWilliams et al., 2006; Spence et al., 2003).

Preuss and Perschke (2010) identified important factors for CSR engagement in SMEs based on the agency theory and the resource-based view: ownership, stakeholders, managerial expertise, organisational structure, and market type. However, regarding the integration of CSR processes, drivers have been identified in existing studies examining the CSR-SME relationship that mainly focus on the stakeholder theory and social capital (Vázquez-Carrasco and López-Pérez, 2013). Preuss and Perschke (2010) confirm that the theoretical conceptualisation of CSR in SMEs is manifested by the stakeholder theory and the social capital model. However, their influence can vary depending on a firm's individual characteristics.

Moreover, Porter and Kramer (2006) argue for a distinction between firms that aim only to reduce potential risk and meet stakeholder expectations (responsive CSR) and those companies actively working to increase positive social and environmental impacts and reduce negative impacts (strategic CSR). These different motivational approaches highlight that the degree of CSR implementation may vary. Moving beyond the responsive (or defensive) approach, strategic CSR allows a firm to choose a unique position, take different actions, improve the relationship between company and society, and integrate CSR into the firm's strategy (Porter and Kramer, 2006). Therefore, the most important theoretical perspectives are helpful to achieving an increased understanding of the CSR concept.

2.3.1 Carroll's Pyramid of CSR

Looking closely on Carroll's model, hierarchy of CSR builds on economic, legal, ethical, and philanthropic responsibilities, which are organised in a pyramid. Economic responsibility is the ground level from which the companies rise to the top of the pyramid, reaching volunteering or philanthropy at the highest level. Carroll's CSR pyramid is illustrated in Figure 1.

Figure 1: Carroll's pyramid of CSR

Source: Adapted from Carroll (2016).

The ground level of the pyramid is formed by economic responsibilities, addressing the purpose of businesses being economic organisations and providing services and goods to demanding customers. Over time, businesses' motivation to earn profits transformed into the maximisation of profits, which has been a driving value ever since (Carroll, 1991). When companies add value, they create profit, and that profit is beneficial for all stakeholders of a business (Carroll, 2016). The required economic responsibility is the foundation of all other business responsibilities (Carroll, 1991). Currently, the global business environment is hypercompetitive, making economic and sustainable topics more important than ever before. A financially and economically unsuccessful business is not likely to survive in the long-term (Carroll, 2016).

Legal responsibilities address the expectation of businesses to comply with regulations and laws initiated by federal, state, and local governments, forming the fundamental rules of business operations. Moreover, the partial fulfilment of a 'social contract' between society and firms includes pursuing economic responsibilities in accordance with the law. Legal responsibilities are codified ethics created by the lawmakers to guarantee basic notions of fair operations. Although legal responsibilities are displayed as a subsequent stage due to historical development, combined with economic responsibilities, they are the foundation of a free enterprise system (Carroll, 1991).

In contrast to legal and economic aspects that represent norms of justice and fairness, ethical responsibilities constitute actions and practices desired or prohibited by members of society not existing in law (Carroll, 2016). These responsibilities include norms, standards, and expectations related to specific conceptions of fairness of employees, consumers, shareholders, and the community or the expectation of how the stakeholders' rights should be protected. The change in ethics or values anticipates the establishment of laws since this change urge the creation of new regulations. For instance, consumer, environmental, or civil rights movements indicated transformations in social values and led to changes in legislation (Carroll, 1991).

Furthermore, ethical responsibility can reflect emerging new norms and values in society, although they meet higher standards and are not yet required by law (Carroll, 2016). Consequently, ethical responsibilities are frequently hard to define and are subject to public discussions, making them difficult for companies to deal with. Over the last decades, ethical responsibility has emerged as a fixed component of CSR and the next layer of the CSR pyramid. Ethical and legal responsibilities are closely connected and affect each other by influencing the legal layer to broaden and increase the pressure on businesses with higher expectations to act more fairly and consciously than required by law (Carroll, 1991).

The top of Carroll's pyramid is philanthropy, meaning businesses can conduct corporate actions that are positively evaluated by society, so the company meets the expectation of being a good corporate citizen. These actions encompass active engagement in contributions to enhance human welfare and are, for example, donations of financial resources or time to promote and support education or arts. In contrast to ethical responsibilities, philanthropic actions are not expected from society in a moral or ethical sense. Society and communities welcome and desire contributions from businesses but do not assess these firms as unethical if they do not deliver the money, facilities, or human resources at the desired level (Carroll, 1991).

Thus, philanthropy is a firm's voluntary decision regardless of the existing expectations of society (Carroll, 2016). The differentiation between philanthropic and ethical responsibility is important because of some businesses' perception that they are socially responsible if they are simply good citizens. Thus, philanthropy is clearly desired, but CSR is not limited to this layer of the pyramid. Instead, the other categories form the foundation of CSR, and philanthropy is a welcomed addition (Carroll, 1991). Table 1 summarises the relevant expectations of economic, legal, and social responsibilities.

Economic Responsibilities	➢ Being profitable ➢ Securing the long-term survival of the business and supporting society
Legal Responsibilities	➢ Acting in a manner consistent with the expectations of government and law ➢ Complying with various federal, state, and local regulations ➢ Behaving as law-abiding corporate citizens ➢ Fulfilling all legal obligations to societal stakeholders ➢ Providing goods and services that meet at least the minimal legal requirements
Ethical Responsibilities	➢ Performing in a manner consistent with expectations of social and ethical norms ➢ Recognising and respecting new or evolving ethical or moral norms adopted by society ➢ Preventing ethical norms from being compromised in order to achieve business goals ➢ Being good corporate citizens by doing what is expected morally or ethically ➢ Recognising that business integrity and ethical behaviour go beyond mere compliance with laws and regulations

Table 1: Expectations of economic, legal and social responsibilities

Source: Adapted from Carroll (2016).

Carroll's CSR pyramid intends to illustrate that CSR in a company consists of different, interconnected components that create a holistic concept (Carroll, 2016). A detailed investigation of the components can help managers gain a deeper understanding of the responsibilities and the dynamic connections between them. From a managerial perspective, a company that engages in CSR should seek to gain profits, obey the law, be ethical, and be a good corporate citizen (Carroll, 1991).

Carroll (2016) summarises that CSR has proved to be solid in both the past and the present. Globalisation, reconciliation with profitability, institutionalisation, an academic proliferation have emerged as main drivers for the development of CSR. Through various practices, CSR has been quickly accepted and conducted regardless of a country's development level. Thus, CSR has emerged as an important management strategy currently integrated into organisational structures, policies, and practices. However, depending on the company's strategy, industry characteristics, the state of economy, management style, and the company's size, the implementation of the responsibilities may vary (Carroll, 1991). In the future, CSR and models like the CSR pyramid will prosper and offer new solutions and strategies for businesses (Carroll, 2016).

A new study by Lu et al. (2020) demonstrated that the incorporation of CSR activities in the SME sector as a business strategy is advisable. The study proved that CSR, as a powerful business strategy, improves organisational performance interconnected with Carroll's CSR pyramid. Due to the global trend and necessity of environmental protection, Lu et al. (2020) suggest adding environmental responsibilities to Carroll's pyramid to meet the emerging expectations.

2.3.2 Stakeholder Theory

2.3.2.1 Main Features of Stakeholder Theory

The stakeholder theory was introduced by Edward Freeman in 1984. Freeman's theory offered a positive view of manager's support of CSR and assumes that managers are in charge for the satisfaction of different constituents who can affect the business' outcomes (McWilliams et al., 2006). Stakeholders are a group that the business needs to exist (Parmar et al., 2010). The literature diverges into a narrow (customers, suppliers, community, shareholders, and employees) and wide (public, special interest groups, and the government) perception of stakeholders (Freeman et al., 2010; Maaß, 2010). The business receives support from the primary stakeholders (narrow view), who are essential for the company to survive, and the business has special duties to this group. In contrast, secondary stakeholders (wide view) do not have a formal claim on the firm, and the management has no special duties to them. However, the company can have moral duties, for example, to avoid harming the stakeholders. Still, the negotiation of the stakeholder status within a company depends on businesses' individual features and is an interesting investigation field (Parmar et al., 2010). Figure 2 depicts the stakeholders from the narrow view in the inner circle and those from the wide perspective in the outer circle.

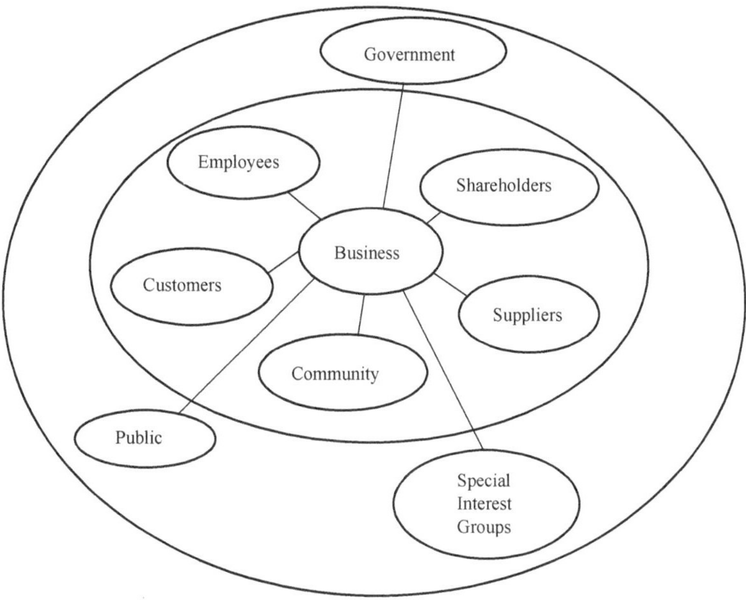

Figure 2: Stakeholders of a business
Source: Own illustration.

Managers need to broaden their view and not only focus on shareholders. Moreover, the company can benefit to engage in CSR activities that are also relevant for non-financial stakeholders, because otherwise they can cancel their support for the business (McWilliams et al., 2006). Here, managers should take the ethical dimension of CSR into account and the business case for involving in these activities (Donaldson and Preston, 1995). Stakeholders holding a stake or interest of the business can have an economic, legal, or ethical nature (Carroll and Brown, 2018). For example, employees or owners can have a legal claim concerning an explicit or implicit contract. Also, interest groups may insist on their moral claim to receive a fair treatment or to pursue their conviction for a business decision (Carroll, 1991). Freeman (2010) explains that the appropriate weighing of stakeholder demands within a company aims to minimise risks regarding these interest groups, which directly or indirectly affect the companies' performance, processes, and success. According to Parmar et al. (2010), the stakeholder management suggests solving the following problems and risks:

- Value creation and trade: How is value created and traded in a rapidly changing and global business context?
- The ethics of capitalism: What are the connections between ethics and capitalism?
- The managerial mindset: How should managers think about management to better create value and explicitly connect business and ethics?

Stakeholder theory proposes that the probability of effectively solving these problems increases if the analysis is based on relationships between a company and groups of individuals who may be or are affected by the problems. The stakeholder perspective assumes that business consists of multiple relationships connected to the business operations. More precisely, business is the way stakeholders and managers communicate to commonly create and trade value. In business, gaining the necessary comprehension of how these relationships work and develop over time is essential. The management is responsible for regulating and shaping the relationships, aiming to create the maximum value for the stakeholders and to appropriately distribute this value (Parmar et al., 2010).

Moreover, stakeholder management not only supports firms' survival and progress in capitalist systems, but it also includes moral considerations regarding values, choices, risks, and opportunities for groups or individuals. Ultimately, a management that focuses on creating, maintaining, and aligning stakeholder relationships enables practitioners to create value and avoid moral mistakes. The stakeholder perspective can be evaluated from a pragmatic viewpoint as a framework, a set of ideas, or a genre of management theory from which other theoretical models can be derived. The applicability is not limited to a specific purpose; instead, the adaptability of stakeholder management means it can be applied in diverse settings and for different aims (Parmar et al., 2010). Practical evidence for the applicability of stakeholder theory is apparent in different disciplines, for example, health care, law, public administration, ethics, and environmental policy (Freeman et al., 2010). The diversity within stakeholder theory led to theoretical suggestions on how stakeholder management can be systematically structured (Parmar et al., 2010). Donaldson and Preston (1995) proposed a four-part classification of research:

- Descriptive: Factual claims about what management and firms do
- Instrumental: Outcomes of specific managerial behaviour
- Normative: Questioning what managers or businesses should do
- Managerial: Addressing the needs of practitioners.

The reason for this division lies in the particular roles and methodologies of each part of stakeholder theory. The descriptive and instrumental classifications rely on social sciences and focus on concrete facts. The normative part focusses on moral questions, which ethicists believe should be the core of the stakeholder perspective (Donaldson and Preston, 1995). However, these sections are interconnected, and there is no justification to sharply separate the stakeholder view into classes and privileged social science investigations. The stakeholder theory should be seen as a unity of different ideas that can act as an aid to managers to create value for stakeholders (Parmar et al., 2010).

2.3.2.2 Limitations of Stakeholder Theory

It is also important to examine boundaries or alternative perceptions regarding the stakeholder theory.

Critics argue that stakeholder theory primarily focuses on the distributions of financial outputs (Marcoux, 2000). Supporters of this view claim that the focus of stakeholder theory is the question of who within a business receives its resources. According to this perspective, an intense conflict between an organisation's stakeholders and shareholders can be a consequence (Parmar et al., 2010). In contrast, stakeholder theorists argue that distribution is not the core of the stakeholder view as process and procedural justice is involved. Also, stakeholder theory supporters claim that stakeholders deserve the right to co-determinate the allocation of resources, that this approach influences how they view the distribution of resources, and the stakeholders' involvement can finally create new chances for value creation. Moreover, stakeholder theorists refer to research that proves that stakeholders tend to accept outcomes when they observe that the process is fair. Additionally, distribution is not only limited to financial resources, but rather information is available and sharable between shareholders and stakeholders without causing conflicts (Phillips et al., 2003).

Further, some critics state that the stakeholder view is an excuse for managerial opportunism (Jensen, 2002; Marcoux, 2000). Supporters of this perspective argue that it becomes easier for managers to engage in self-interest because they can justify their actions due to the greater number of interest groups they are dealing with. This problem would not appear if the sole focus was on shareholders (Parmar et al., 2010). The reaction from stakeholder theorists embodies two core arguments. Much managerial opportunism has been conducted in connection with shareholder maximisation, for instance, by Enron and Worldcom. Al Dunlap is presented as example for mismanaging firms by aiming to maximise his own financial benefits (Parmar et al., 2010). Further, this criticism is an issue for many other theories of organisation and is not only intended for stakeholder theory (Phillips et al., 2003).

Another criticism is that stakeholders should be treated equally (Marcoux, 2000). Although different versions of equal stakeholder management have been delivered (e.g., egalitarianism), critics concentrate on the notion of treating stakeholders equally. Here, discussions address appropriate stakeholder management and a balance in related actions (Parmar et al., 2010). According to Phillips et al. (2003), theorists found useful and relevant classifications of stakeholders, enabling the organisations to make suitable decisions regarding their understanding of the stakeholder view and their individual situation and circumstances. Parmar et al. (2010) add that this assessment is related to the previously introduced assumption that the stakeholder view is limited to distributions of financial outputs. Instead, the focus lies on the considerations and the process of decision making.

Moreover, critics argue that stakeholder theory requires adaptation to current law (Hendry, 2001). This claim is based on the consideration that laws need to be adapted to simplify the application of stakeholder theory or to ensure the legality of stakeholder management (Parmar et al., 2010). For instance, critics argue that stakeholder theory supports the introduction of laws that force the management to pursue stakeholder interests (Humber, 2002). However, the main argument against this criticism is that stakeholder theory does not include requirements to change the law allowing businesses to apply it. Although there may be reasons to consider a change in legislation, they are not compulsory in the stakeholder theory. When legal considerations become law, they may prove useful. Nevertheless, they must not be confused with the core of stakeholder theory or be perceived as essential to applying the theory (Parmar et al., 2010).

Further, a criticism is that stakeholder theory refers to the whole economy and has socialist characteristics (Barnett, 1997). The term 'stakeholder economy' is sometimes used in parts of the UK and Europe (Parmar et al., 2010). However, Phillips et al. (2003) clearly state that stakeholder theory refers to organisations and is not a theory of political economy. Further, stakeholder theory emerged as concept of voluntary exchange for individuals in a capitalistic system. Thus, the argument of socialism contradicts the concept of stakeholder theory (Parmar et al., 2010).

The last criticism is that stakeholder theory is a moral doctrine (Orts and Strudler, 2002). A morale doctrine may address the full array of moral issues that come along without reference to any other theory (Rawls, 1993). However, Phillips et al. (2003) argue that stakeholder theory can be classified as a theory of organisations encompassing issues for businesses. Moreover, this theory is not capable of covering all relevant issues for companies, and obviously, it is not possible for stakeholder theory to address all the moral questions in the world.

Like the majority of theories, stakeholder theory is a tool to gain a better understanding and decision support in a complex world. Stakeholder theory, like any tool, has benefits and weaknesses. This stakeholder perspective is especially helpful in solving the three problems addressed earlier (Parmar et al., 2010).

2.3.2.3 CSR and Stakeholder Theory

Corporate social responsibility is an important area of interest concerning stakeholder theory. Over the years, different concepts related to CSR emerged: corporate social responsiveness (Ackerman, 1975), corporate social performance (Carroll, 1979), corporate citizenship (Waddock, 2004), corporate governance (Freeman and Evan, 1990), corporate social entrepreneurship (Austin et al., 2006), sustainability, and the triple bottom line (Elkington, 1997). For example, the triple bottom line framework stresses the importance of three pillars for which a firm should be economically, socially, and environmentally responsible: profit, people, and planet. CSR is closely connected to the triple bottom line framework, and a firm's attention to all three features causes sustainable results for CSR activities (Księżak and Fischbach, 2017).

All the mentioned concepts aim to widen the duties of businesses. Therefore, these concepts do not focus exclusively on financial matters but, instead, on the broader company purpose and on the delivery of those aims. The stakeholder view is helpful in CSR research to empirically and conceptually recognise and specify social obligations. Moreover, capabilities and concepts of CSR are based on a separation of social interests, ethics, and business. Thus, CSR is limited to solving the problems addressed by stakeholder theory. More precisely, value creation and trade are barely embodied by the CSR concept because ethics appears to be considered an afterthought in the process of value creation (Parmar et al., 2010).

When integrating social responsibility with a company's existing economic and financial responsibility, CSR intensifies the problem of ethics and capitalism. The financial crisis in 2008/2009 illustrates that the separation of ethics and capitalism in large financial services and banks had negative consequences. These organisations all had CSR programs and policies, but did not recognise the connection between their actions, ethics, and the creation of value. Thus, they could not satisfy expectations or fulfil their responsibilities to their stakeholders. These circumstances led to the destruction of value for the whole organisation (Parmar et al., 2010). Research conducted in this area claimed that the world has significant social problems that need attention. Moreover, the existing tension between social and financial demands on a business requires further investigation (Margolis and Walsh, 2003). Parmar et al. (2010) argue that business actions have an independent blend of moral and financial effects, which affect the stakeholder. Thus, a distinction between social and financial issues cannot be made. Margolis and Walsh (2003) said that the goal is to craft role and purpose for the company that builds internal coherence among competing and incommensurable duties, objectives, and concerns. This statement can be interpreted as the manager's task to balance stakeholder interests (Parmar et al., 2010).

2.3.2.4 Business Strategy and Stakeholder Influence

The business strategy is directed toward a firm's economic performance. Stakeholder theory covers economic and social business aspects and offers enough reasons to declare the link between higher economic performance and stakeholder management. Here are some examples:

- The avoidance of negative outcomes and the reduction of risks leads to more stable predictable returns (Graves and Waddock, 1994).

- Mutually beneficial stakeholder relationships can improve a business's capacity to create wealth. However, a failure in these relationships can lead to limitations in a firm's wealth-creation capacity (Post et al., 2002).
- In the marketplace, excellent reputations attract more potential business partners, customers and employees (Puncheva, 2008).
- Stakeholder management is a source of competitive advantage because the company has more and better business opportunities from which to choose (Harrison et al., 2010).
- Stakeholders are more likely to reveal meaningful information that can cause increased efficiency and innovation (Harrison et al., 2010).

- Good stakeholder relationships enable a company to achieve excellent financial performance in the long-term. Moreover, poorly performing businesses improve their performance more quickly with the help of good stakeholder relationships (Choi and Wang, 2009).

Concentrating future investigations on the employed strategies that address a wide range of stakeholders is advisable. While the stakeholder view recognises that the business and the stakeholders have a two-way-relationship, many investigations have focussed on the company's management of its stakeholders and its strategies. However, the interest in the influence of stakeholders on a business's strategy has strongly increased (Parmar et al., 2010). There is a close, even 'natural' connection between stakeholders and CSR. Defining 'social' in CSR resulted in some disagreement or vagueness because the clear addressees of the business' responsibility were lacking. The stakeholder model directs the social responsibility to clearly defined interest groups and thus helping the company to orientate (Carroll, 1991).

Welge et al. (2017) add that it can be expedient for companies to give preferential treatment to selected stakeholder groups depending on their power and market position. Stakeholder management is pluralistic in terms of interests and can, therefore, be selective and strategy orientated. However, the academic discussion is divided regarding adequate prioritisation of specific stakeholders (Hungenberg, 2014). Urgency, legitimacy, and power have been identified as criteria of stakeholders, making it possible to evaluate the stakeholders' meaningfulness for the company (Mitchell et al., 1997; Mitchell et al., 2011). Figure 3 illustrates the widely recognised stakeholder classification by Mitchell et al. (1997).

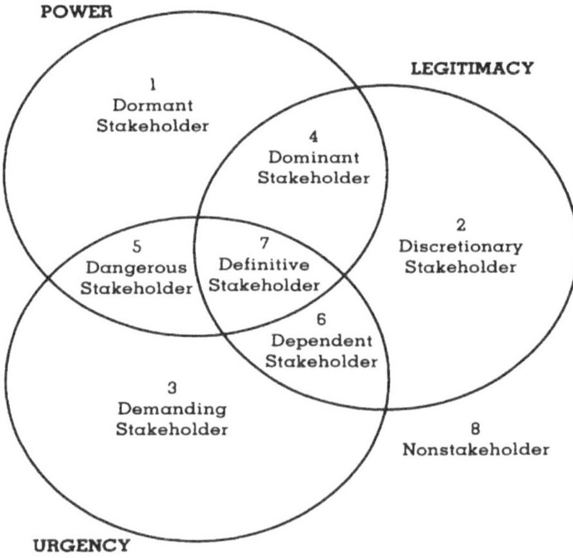

Figure 3: Stakeholder classification
Source: Mitchell et al. (1997).

The following description of the stakeholder identification and salience relies on Mitchell et al. (1997). The foundation of this concept is based on three assumptions. First, managers aim to achieve goals and pay attention to different kinds of stakeholders. Second, the perspective of managers defines the stakeholder salience. Salience can be understood as the degree to which managers prioritise competing stakeholder claims. Third, the classification of stakeholders is based on the existence/possession of at least one of the tree attributes (power, legitimacy, urgency). Power is the relationship among social actors in which one actor can get another social actor to do something that he would not done before. Legitimacy is a generalised perception or assumption the actions of an entity are proper, desirable, or appropriate in the frame of socially constructed system of values, norms and definitions. Urgency describes the degree to which stakeholder claims call for immediate attention. This model proposes that stakeholder 'salience will be positively related to the cumulative number of stakeholder attributes – power, legitimacy, and urgency – perceived by managers to be present' (Mitchell et al., 1997: 873).

Areas 1, 2 and 3 are featured with low salience having the possession of only one attribute. As visible in Figure 3, dormant, discretionary, and demanding stakeholders possess only one attribute. The possession of two attributes (areas 4, 5 and 6) makes stakeholders more salient and they 'expect something'. The stakeholder groups here are dominant, dangerous, and dependent stakeholders. The presence of all three attributes (area 7) makes a stakeholder highly salient, and these stakeholders are called definitive. The following overview gives an about the different stakeholder classes including attributes, main features and examples (Mitchell et al., 1997).

Possession of one attribute

According to Mitchell et al. (1997:874), stakeholder 'salience will be low where only one of the stakeholder attributes – power, legitimacy, and urgency – is perceived by managers to be present'.

The first class of stakeholders possessing only one attribute (power) are dormant stakeholders. These stakeholders use their power to pursue their will on a company, but without having an urgent claim or a legitimate right, the power cannot be used. The interaction between dormant stakeholders and a business are minimal or non-existent. Nevertheless, they have the potential to obtain a second attribute that management should consider. The relationship between the stakeholder and management has a dynamic nature, and if dormant stakeholders acquire urgency or legitimacy, the management should be prepared to react appropriately. Here are some examples: a person that can spend a lot of money; somebody who is able to influence the medial attention; fired employees can be dormant stakeholders aiming to extent their power (Mitchell et al., 1997).

Discretionary stakeholders' main attribute is legitimacy. Despite possessing legitimacy, these stakeholders cannot pursue their desires because they lack power and urgent claims. This class of stakeholders is especially relevant for CSR and performance research. Referring to Carroll (1991), discretionary stakeholders are most likely to be recipients of corporate philanthropy. The absence of urgency and power means there is no necessity for managers to engage in an active relationship with these stakeholders, but they can do so. Discretionary stakeholders can be non-profit organisations like schools, hospitals, and soup kitchens, receiving donations and volunteer labour from firms.

Demanding stakeholders' attribute is urgency. They are characterised by urgent claims without having power or legitimacy and are perceived by management as a disruptive, but non-dangerous, factor. These stakeholders are bothersome, tiresome, and achieve little to no management attention. When stakeholders are unwilling or unable to obtain legitimacy or power to develop the saliency of their claims, urgency is not enough to be heard as a stakeholder. An example is a lone picketer demonstrating in front of a firm's headquarters with a sign saying that the end is near because of the firm's products, which may cause some confusion to the managers, but nothing more (Mitchell et al., 1997).

Possession of two attributes

According to Mitchell et al. (1997:876), stakeholder 'salience will be moderate where two of the stakeholder attributes – power, legitimacy, and urgency – are perceived by managers to be present'.

The first class of stakeholders possessing two attributes (power and legitimacy) are dominant stakeholders. These stakeholders are characterised as dominant because they hold legitimate claims and the ability to act on these expectations. These legitimate and powerful claims should receive management's attention. The combination of these two attributes is assumed to create some formal mechanism acknowledging the relevance of the stakeholders' relationships with the company. The company usually has an investor relations office to communicate with important investors. There are also often departments to handle the relationship with significant creditors, community leaders, and others. A human resources department manages the relationship between employees and the company. Moreover, a company delivers different reports addressing powerful, legitimate stakeholders. These reports are, for example, annual reports, proxy statements, CSR reports, and environmental reports (Mitchell et al., 1997).

Dependent stakeholders possess the attributes urgency and legitimacy. Urgent and legitimate claims make stakeholders dependent because they depend on other stakeholders or the management. In this constellation, power is not mutual, and its exercise is regulated by the advocacy or guardianship of other stakeholders or the guidance of internal managerial values. The satisfaction of the claims is connected to the benevolence and voluntarism of the business's management or to the advocacy of powerful stakeholders. For example, in 1989, the giant oil spill caused by the oil tanker Exxon Valdez in Alaska led to fatal consequences for the environment. Local residents, marine birds and mammals, and the environment itself were affected. These stakeholder groups had legitimate and urgent claims, but their lack of power to enforce their claims hindered them. The enforcement of these claims was realised when the Alaska state government and court system (dominant stakeholders) provided guardianship for the dependant stakeholders. Through this support the dependant stakeholders became the most salient stakeholder class because the urgent claims were adopted and enforced by the dominant stakeholders. This stakeholder classification clearly incorporates dynamic relationships (Mitchell et al., 1997). A similar situation appeared during the Deepwater Horizon oil spill in 2010, which was an industrial disaster in the Gulf of Mexico.

Dangerous stakeholders' attributes are urgency and power. They are coercive and potentially violent, making them dangerous to the organisation. Their lack of legitimacy often leads to coercive power. These stakeholders possibly endanger the stakeholder-management relationship, as well as both parties' well-being and lives. Therefore, identifying these stakeholders is vital because not doing so could lead to a failure to reduce the danger level, and appropriate hazard preparation would be hindered. The identification must not be mistaken for acknowledging dangerous stakeholders; instead, it offers the opportunity to minimise risks and maintain civility and civilisation. Examples for dangerous stakeholders are employee sabotage, wildcat strikes, terrorism (religious or political groups utilising shootings or kidnappings aimed to create attention for their claims), or environmentalists spiking trees in areas to be logged (Mitchell et al., 1997).

Possession of three attributes

According to Mitchell et al. (1997:878), stakeholder 'salience will be high where all three of the stakeholder attributes – power, legitimacy, and urgency – are perceived by managers to be present'.

Definitive stakeholders possess all three attributes. As presented, a stakeholder holding powerful and legitimate claims is a dominant stakeholder and requires managerial attention. When this stakeholder's claim is extended by the attribute of urgency, the management can immediately react and prioritise this claim. Furthermore, other stakeholders possessing two attributes can become definitive stakeholders if they obtain the third attribute. An insufficient or inappropriate approach to definite stakeholders can negatively affect the management and even cause an exchange or removal in these positions. Therefore, an accurate perception of the three attributes is vital. Moreover, acknowledging and reacting to the implication of salience is necessary. In addition, it is important to understand that inattention to or misperception of the definitive stakeholders' claims can have serious consequences. For instance, stockholders with significant shares are definitive stakeholders.

This concept enables the management to conduct a systematic sorting of the relationships between managers and stakeholders because these relationships attain and relinquish salience in the businesses' dynamics. Moreover, with the help of this model, managers can map the legitimacy of stakeholders and thus become more sensitive to the moral implications of their actions regarding each stakeholder. Therefore, this concept initiates and supports normative thought in managerial actions. Overall, stakeholder theory considers the three attributes power, urgency, and legitimacy independently from the potentially unsettling results. The management must be able to identify and recognise the relevant groups that hold power in the business environment and intend to impose their will. Further, power and urgency should be examined if management aims to implement the legal and moral claims of legitimate stakeholders (Mitchell et al., 1997).

Investigating other argumentations regarding business strategy and stakeholder influence, Carroll (1991) states that, from the CSR perspective, legitimacy is the most important criterion; however, from a managerial view, power is the most relevant. Legitimacy encompasses the extent to which an interest group's claim is justifiable. For instance, a few hundred employees who will be dismissed due to a plant's downsizing decision have a more legitimate claim to managerial attention than a local association concerned about losing a charity sponsor. Regarding stakeholder's power, there are some major differences. For example, an unorganised group of small investors have far less opportunities and power over management decisions than large institutional investors due to the small investors' organisation and amount of investment. Managers must balance the business's targets and the stakeholders' claims while fulfilling the company's most relevant stakeholder expectations and simultaneously complying with other stakeholders' interests. It is unlikely to fully satisfy all parties involved in the stakeholder management process, but it is still a desirable direction to achieve long-term goals (Carroll, 1991). According to Carroll (1991), the following questions aim to describe, understand, analyse, and manage stakeholder relationships:

- Who are the stakeholders?
- What are the stakeholders' stakes, interests, claims, and expectations?
- What chances and difficulties are presented by the stakeholders?

- What economic, legal, ethical, and philanthropic responsibility does the business have to the stakeholders?
- Which strategies, decisions, or actions should the business realise to best deal with these responsibilities?

According to Carroll's pyramid, stakeholder groups can be assigned to the four responsibilities. Economic responsibilities are especially relevant for employees and shareholders due to their interest in the business's financial stability and prosperity. Next, legal responsibility is now not only relevant to the owners of a business but to consumers and employees because of the increasing tendency to litigate against companies. Further, ethical responsibilities are represented in all stakeholder groups, and frequently, employees, the environment, and customers are encountered during examinations of ethical business issues. Last, the stakeholder group's community, non-profit organisations, and employees are usually involved in the business's philanthropic responsibilities (Carroll, 2016).

2.3.2.5 Stakeholder Management in SMEs

Russo and Perrini (2010) argue that since SMEs do not aim to maximise profits, a company's success is measured with quality indicators evaluating their relationship with stakeholders. Garriga and Melé (2004) add that firms must generate long-term value to ensure survival and are responsible for their activities within a social environment. Moreover, Maaß et al. (2014) demonstrate that a firm's target is to reduce costs, which is connected to the stakeholders' demands. Thus, as Sachs and Ruhli (2005) emphasise, CSR activities should concentrate on communication with interest groups to identify their concerns and react with suitable activities. Due to the SMEs' size, it is vital to categorise the importance of the SMEs' stakeholders and thus the possibly conflicting stakeholder interests (Maaß, 2010). SMEs tend to focus on the satisfaction of internal stakeholders (e.g., employees) (Jamali et al., 2009). Moreover, stakeholder management is primary economically orientated, but CSR also covers social and environmental aspects. Also, the stakeholder approach is especially useful for SMEs due to their often-fixed position in the supply chain and thus the need to meet the claims of the interest groups. Furthermore, suggestions regarding the implementation of CSR in German SMEs are limited to the explanation of possible instruments. Therefore, the stakeholder approach would be a valid starting point to solve this issue (Maaß et al., 2014). However, other authors (Jenkins, 2004; Perrini, 2006) doubt the suitability of the stakeholder approach for SMEs because of differences between the management styles of managers of large businesses and the owner-influenced decision making within SMEs.

2.3.3 Social Capital

2.3.3.1 Main Features of Social Capital

As outlined, the stakeholder theory can be beneficial for the implementation of CSR in SMEs, but this theory has weak points. An additional perspective, social capital, has been studied in the context of CSR in SMEs in different locations, including Germany (Spence et al., 2003).

Social capital is related to the productive value of social connections. The term 'productive' encompasses two dimensions: the production of market goods and services and the production of a broad range of well-being outcomes. Social capital enables a more comprehensive understanding that human relations and norms of behaviour have an instrumental value benefiting different aspects of life. Implementing a social aspect into the analysis of the way that economic and other well-being outcomes are generated seems rational. Social norms of behaviour and relationships have a relevant role when shaping individual and common well-being outcomes. This idea is recognised by social capital, making it possible to implement the value of social relationships into analytical models. Measures of social interaction include the frequency of socialising or trust in other people. These measures have been connected to various outcomes, for example, individual happiness, government performance or health status. In particular, the links between measures of social capital and economic performance have gained attention. Despite the high interest in social capital, and similar concepts, there is no existing uniform definition and measurement of this term. Social capital has been used in various situations covering different themes and tensions that indicate the directions in which social capital is applied. The different perspectives were influenced by Bourdieu, Coleman, and Putnam (Scrivens and Smith, 2013).

Bourdieu's understanding of social capital is directed to networks. Specifically, the focus lies on the payoff from network membership regarding access to resources and possibilities including exclusionary, private aspects of goods incorporated in personal networks. This approach has affected research dealing with the connections between micro-level networks and positive individual results, especially in the area of professional advancement and labour market status (Scrivens and Smith, 2013).

Coleman argued that social capital is defined by its functions and, therefore, is applicable to a much wider range of situations. This perspective includes micro-level and meso-level networks involving the role of community relationships, norms, and sanctions on group outcomes and the role of interactions within families on individual outcomes, like educational attainment. The micro-level addresses family, school, organisations, and interpersonal networks. The meso-level can include communities, neighbourhoods, or business clusters. The importance of both private and public goods is acknowledged in this view. Nevertheless, Coleman noticed that networks can have a harmful effect (e.g., devaluation of academic achievements), and in these cases, social capital must be treated with caution (Scrivens and Smith, 2013).

Putnam believed social capital on the macro- and meso-levels of society and emphasised that social capital is a public good. The macro-level refers to regions or countries. Putnam defined social capital as specific features of social life, especially networks, norms, and trust, which encourage participants to behave more effectively and enforce common aims. He attributed networks of civic engagement, trust, and norms of reciprocity to social capital (Scrivens and Smith, 2013).

One main disagreement about the social capital concept is the question of whether social capital is a private or public good. In the first case, social capital is understood as a resource for individuals at a micro-level and explains how people access help and opportunities through network memberships. The second case addresses social capital as a resource for achieving cooperation among the group and generating benefits on a societal level. The literature delivered many possible definitions mainly focussing either on the first or the second case (Scrivens and Smith, 2013). Regarding the different perspectives on social capital, Scrivens and Smith (2013) structured the approaches and delivered an overview of the possible interpretations of the term.

	Network Structure and Activities	**Productive Resources**
Individual	Personal Relationships	Social Network Support
Collective	Civic Engagement	Cooperative Norms and Trust

Table 2: Interpretation of social capital
Source: Adapted from Scrivens and Smith (2013).

Table 2 presents a classification of social capital in four categories. The private activities and outcomes are displayed in the upper row (individual). The bottom row provides public activities and outcomes (collective). The column Network Structure and Activities addresses the structure of networks and the activities creating and maintaining them. The column Productive Resources refers to the types of resources and outcomes generated by networks. These interpretations are legitimate, but they all focus on different phenomena, are supported on different theoretical frameworks about outcomes and drivers, aim to answer different questions, and have different approaches for measurement (Scrivens and Smith, 2013).

Personal relationships are concerned with people's networks and behaviour in society that support establishing and maintaining networks. Such activities include exchanging news by phone or email or spending time with other people. Here, the structure, extent, density, and components of the individual's societal networks are the most important aspects (Scrivens and Smith, 2013).

The nature of people's personal relationships results in social network support and is related to resources available to the individuals through their social networks. These resources may be materially practical, emotional, financial, intellectual, or professional. The quality and strength of the network support may heavily influence the economic and individual social outcomes. The emphasis in this category is on the support that individuals receive and concentrates on questions referring to the causes and results of being able to receive this support (Scrivens and Smith, 2013).

Civic engagement addresses the activities enabling people to contribute to community and civic life, for instance, political participation, volunteering, and group membership. This category focuses on the extent and nature of collective activities. Here, the impact of civic engagement on other outcomes and the identification of drivers of civic engagement are core parts of the analyses (Scrivens and Smith, 2013).

The last category, trust and cooperative norms, is concerned with social norms, trust, and shared values that support social functioning and enable beneficial cooperation. The basis of this category forms the intangible factors incorporated in people's expectations and social norms contributing to better economic and social results. The main concern is to identify the elements of the informal structure and the functioning of society that have a productive role and refers both to social and economic terms. This category is an enabler of collective action (collective resource) and is useful in the context of relevant outcomes of government policy, like government performance or economic growth (Scrivens and Smith, 2013).

2.3.3.2 Limitations of Social Capital

Some critics do not agree with Putnam's argument that social engagement is eroding. Instead, they replace 'eroding' with 'evolving'. Social engagement is changing. People were used to joining groups in the neighbourhood, but now they tend to engage in groups that share their beliefs and interests, for example, environmental protection or gay rights. These groups may exist in the 'real' world, like Greenpeace; however, more social exchange happens online where people never meet physically but still create communities (OECD, 2009).

Another point of criticism is that there is no agreement about the term 'social capital'; there is no exact measurement, and social capital may not even exist. The argumentation states that capital is connected to some form of sacrifice in the present (e.g., studying to achieve future gains) (OECD, 2009). However, as presented, there is sufficient justification that social capital is a relevant versatile concept that can be applied and measured in various situations (Scrivens and Smith, 2013).

2.3.3.3 Social Capital in SMEs

Networks have a significant impact on SMEs, and evidence for this impact is the firm embeddedness of SMEs in their local communities through the relationships between owner and staff and the connectedness of the company with the region (Habisch, 2004; Murillo and Lozano, 2006). Spence et al. (2003) argue that since SMEs are often owner-managed, social capital can lead to positive outcomes, like the stabilisation of mutual expectations and trust, access to local knowledge and information, improvement of the company's reputation, and risk management and insurance. Moreover, Fisher et al. (2009) explain that SMEs tend to emphasise local activities, promote collaboration and dialogue in networked environments, and have well-developed systems to maximise social capital. The German Mittelstand provides evidence through its embeddedness in the region and the managers' intrinsic motivation to contribute to the welfare of the local community (Heblich and Gold, 2008).

However, there are challenges when building social capital: the time-consuming building process, additional costs, and unbalanced problem-solving approaches due to set norms (Nahapiet and Ghoshal, 1998). Lepoutre and Heene (2006) provide empirical evidence that SMEs, in contrast to large companies, do not need public reporting of their CSR activities; instead, accountability is measured by recognition within the networks and social approval. The implementation of CSR should consider talents and strengths to maximise social capital (Fisher et al., 2009). The social capital approach complements the stakeholder view concerning an SME's specific management style. Preuss and Perschke (2010) argue that CSR and social capital complement each other because CSR represents an organisation-level approach to address social and environmental externalities of economic actions. Social capital addresses the company's relationship to actors within or outside the organisation. For instance, empirical evidence (Abel-Koch, 2017) indicates that many German firms conduct socially responsible activities around employees' working conditions, sustainable resources, support of social projects, and climate protection supporting the local social surroundings. German SMEs concentrate on intense contact with employees, suppliers, and customers and employ flexible, long-term orientated structures that enable them to implement an appropriate CSR strategy (Pott et al., 2017). Weiß (2005) states that employee involvement in the enterprises' decision-making is a powerful feature of German businesses. Consequently, SMEs' close relationship to their regional surroundings helps anchor social values in the firms' strategies and realise these values more credibly than large companies (Jonker et al., 2011). Therefore, both stakeholder theory and social capital play a vital role in the everyday business environment of German SMEs.

Russo and Perrini (2010) found that, although SMEs can act responsibly due to relationships, openness, and trust, they do not exploit these benefits based on their social capital. Thus, a focused stakeholder approach can support SMEs in managing their opportunities more effectively and achieving benefits through their organised CSR engagement. Existing studies, like Von Weltzien and Shankar (2011), Perrini (2006), Weber (2008), and Jenkins (2006), have demonstrated that CSR is beneficial for SMEs for the following reasons: reputation improvement, long-term cost reduction, attraction and retention of qualified workforce, growth opportunities, profit increases, better market positioning, personal owner's/manager's satisfaction, competitive advantage, and much more. These aspects should be considered by the SMEs' management, evaluated by relevance, weighted against the available resources, and wisely implemented (Von Weltzien and Shekar, 2011). In addition, they can act as a company's motivational factors and potential goals. According to Sen and Bhattacharya (2001), the company's choice of activities to realise the goals can be divided into the following categories: community support, diversity, employee support, environment, non-domestic operation, and products.

2.3.4 Total Responsibility Management

Thus far, different determining factors were addressed for the CSR engagement in SMEs, and Waddock et al. (2002) provided a useful theoretical model interconnecting them.

Waddock et al. (2002) argue that modern companies face pressure from stakeholders and institutional organisations, demanding increased responsibility from them. Therefore, businesses need to respond strategically to competitive pressures and develop their management systems. This approach enables companies to react to pressures for responsibility, satisfy stakeholder demands, and create a long-lasting interactive relationship with stakeholders. The foundation of successful responsibility management within a company is positive stakeholder relationships.

The total responsibility management framework (TRM) involves three components: inspiration, integration, and innovation/improvement. Inspiration refers to vision and goal setting, appropriate leadership, and management; integration addresses the suitable implementation of the responsibility vision into concrete processes, practices, and employee relationships; and innovation involves the control mechanisms aimed to create improvement. These components are related to stakeholder and social pressure, meaning that the demands of these interest groups should be fulfilled. The TRM by Waddock et al. (2002) is illustrated in Figure 4.

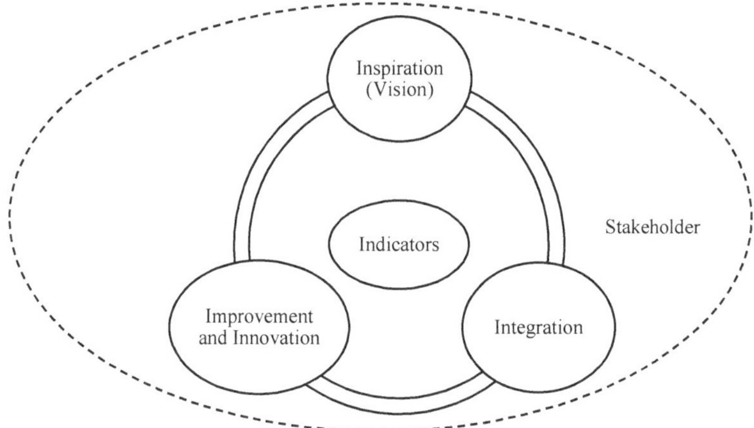

Figure 4: Total responsibility management framework

Source: Adapted from Waddock et al. (2002).

The first key element, inspiration, suggests that responsibility should be implemented into the corporate vision and associated values. In this regard, the top management must not only make a serious commitment to responsible practices and values, but also ensure that everyone in the company and its supply chain is conscious of this commitment and aims to meet it. The institutionalisation of responsibility is not just internal to the firm and directed exclusively downward; instead, the realisation of this process includes an upward and downward perspective within the firm and its suppliers. Moreover, communication regarding the explicit commitment to responsible practice should be regularly addressed, enabling the company to integrate the vision throughout the firm (Waddock et al., 2002).

Integration is the next aspect in the TRM framework, including the realisation of the responsibility vision with the help of strategies, practices, and specific measurement systems. Companies have often established a department responsible for the execution of responsibility plans. The tasks can include the coordination of responsibility policies, the implementation of (behavioural) codices, the communication of policies and practices to stakeholders, as well as the adjustment and maintenance of these codices. The success of the responsibility management is built on the right implementations on the operational level, meaning that clear systems, structures, and processes are required (Waddock et al., 2002).

The final part of the TRM is improvement, innovation and learning. The main requirement for a company to develop positively is to learn from its mistakes and make improvements. Therefore, the business needs new forms of assessment and measurement, allowing the transparent provision of feedback to stakeholders, who are waiting for information about corporate activities. Also, management and employees are seeking to receive information about the firm's performance. When systems are externally audited, monitored, and reported in accordance with suggestions from the Global Reporting Initiative (GRI), the reliability, credibility, and validity of these data are improved. As mentioned, the communication of a firm's responsible practices is crucial if the company aims to avoid problems and can be realised through instances like public relations, investor relations, marketing, and community relations systems (Waddock et al., 2002).

A company needs indicators to measure its progress and performance in meeting its responsibility goals. These indicators are required in all three parts of the TRM. The measurement and management systems need to at least deliver data for economic, social, and environmental reporting that can be of stakeholder interest. There is a huge pressure on firms to publish the results of responsibility audits and use external auditors. Measurement, information, and reward systems must be part of reporting systems and be reconnected to management; thus, the data can help enhance future actions. The pressure derives from demands related to integrity, respect, standards, transparency, and accountability. Integrity addresses stakeholder demands directed at the honesty of companies. Additionally, stakeholders demand that enterprises adhere to their values and codes, be honest and healthy, and sound relevant to specific stakeholders, as well as the reality of the business's actions and influence should be consistent with its rhetoric. Respect embodies that the stakeholders demand the firm's relationships with stakeholders are engaged and interactive, and that different perspectives are considered in decision-making. Further, standards refer to the stakeholders' demand that communicated values must be turned to action and, at least, internationally agreed values, for instance, human rights and working conditions, are reached. Through transparency, stakeholders require openness about the business's performance regarding economic, social, and environmental impacts. Stakeholders demand accountability for companies to acknowledge their effects and take responsibility for them. Overall, integrity encompass all the explained stakeholder demands (Waddock et al., 2002).

2.3.5 Conceptual Framework

Overall, this chapter addressed important theoretical lenses in connection with determining factors for CSR engagement in SMEs, first providing a conception of CSR by Carroll (1991). Moreover, the motivation/potential, benefits/goals and challenges were addressed by the different studies. The stakeholder theory and social capital refer to the integration process of CSR as well as values for governing the business and CSR. Further, Waddock et al. (2002) developed determining factors for CSR implementation (vision/motivation, integration process) and added the improvement processes and outcome control to the considerations.

Figure 5 presents the conceptual framework demonstrating a comprehensive synthesis of theories, concepts, and schools of thought useful to answering the research question. Stakeholders (stakeholder theory) and the social environment (social capital) influence the decision-making of Mittelstand-companies, thus affecting their CSR approach. Firms planning to engage in CSR must be aware of potential benefits, be motivated, set goals, and consider challenges in the implementation process. Here, a company must prioritise and decide on certain CSR activities aiming to reach its goals. During the whole process, appropriate communication is compulsory to maximise results and avoid misinformation. Moreover, the firm installs controls and analyses the results of its CSR engagement to ensure correct conduct. Here, communication concerning the results is significant to provide information about the degree of stakeholder demand fulfilment. After the analysis, the company can rethink its awareness and motivation and refine its goals. This process leads to changes in Mittelstand-companies' CSR-approach and, in the long run, to a steady development from which a trend can be derived. A firm's individual situation might be dependent on size, industry, region, and management approach. Taken together, the literature indicates that the main determining factors of CSR engagement in SMEs are awareness, motivation/goals, activities, challenges, and communication. These factors were analysed to determine the development of CSR engagement in Mittelstand-firms.

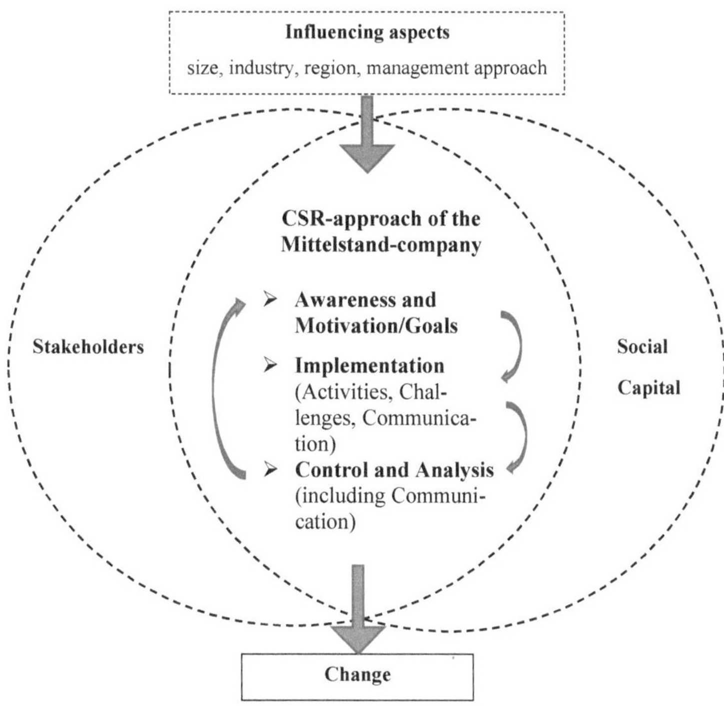

Figure 5: Conceptual framework
Source: Own illustration.

As CSR has gained importance, the necessity for SMEs has arisen to realise a successful CSR implementation. Due to the different characteristics of businesses, especially their sizes, the influence of companies' interest groups differs. Consequently, the determining factors of CSR engagement reflect these conditions. Therefore, it is of interest to determine the development of the key factors of CSR engagement, enabling conclusions about trends. The German Mittelstand is the backbone of the German economy. Thus, this sector would highly benefit from solid advice and implementation direction because many companies want to engage in CSR but do not know how to realise it (Pott et al., 2017).

3. Research Design

3.1 The Research Onion

The book's research design is presented with the help of the 'research onion', which includes six dimensions: philosophy, approach to theory development, methodological choice, strategy, time horizon, and data collection and data analysis (Saunders et al., 2019).

Philosophy
This research adopts the philosophical position of pragmatism, thus focusing on the outlined problem and aiming to contribute to practical solutions (Saunders and Lewis, 2012). Reality is relevant to pragmatists as practical effects of ideas and solutions that inform future practices. As the CSR-SME relationship is a relevant and underdeveloped research area, this practice-orientated and problem-solving philosophy allows for the use of methods most suitable to answer the research question (Saunders et al., 2019).

Approach to Theory Development
The inductive approach is appropriate to answer a research question and add aspects to an existing theory with the research's results. An element of deduction is applied by reviewing the significant academic literature that contributes to the theoretical basis of the research. An inductive theory development from systematic empirical research is characterised by its plausibility, practice-orientation, and accessibility (Saunders and Lewis, 2012),

Methodological Choice
This book analyses the development of German Mittelstand CSR engagement by determining the changes within the key factors and their sub-aspects. According to Taneja et al. (2011), CSR-related studies have been mostly exploratory and descriptive, incorporating a quantitative, qualitative, or mixed-method approach. As in most of the management and business investigations, a range of methods was utilised. However, Vázquez-Carrasco and López-Pérez (2013) found that, in the CSR in SME context, conceptual studies and qualitative methodology are dominant. Although qualitative studies provide in-depth understanding, the results deliver non-standardised data that generally requires classification into categories. In contrast, the quantitative approach ensures that the methods used to collect data are rigorously structured and defined. The results are usually numerical and

standardised data, and analyses are conducted using diagrams and statistics (Saunders et al., 2019). This book employed the quantitative mono-method, which was useful because quantifiable data is essential to determine changes and trends of CSR engagement in Mittelstand-firms.

Strategy

This book analyses the development of CSR engagement within ten years and, therefore, exploits data from existing surveys. This strategy tends to be employed in descriptive and exploratory studies that thoroughly examine a current situation and archive new insights. In addition, surveys are comparatively easy to understand and to explain by analysing the data with the help of descriptive and inferential statistics (Saunders et al., 2019). Moreover, surveys enable standardised data collection from a large number of respondents, allowing easy comparison by using, for example, questionnaires and structured interviews (Saunders and Lewis, 2012). Four large-scale surveys (Gilde GmbH, 2007; Bertelsmann Stiftung 2007; EY, 2012; Pott et al., 2017) were chosen dealing with CSR engagement and the determining factors within Mittelstand-companies. These secondary data are discussed in the next section.

Time Horizon

The utilised surveys were ad hoc, represented a topic at a particular time, and were specific in their subject matter. Although this is an excellent method of examining the current situation, this approach does not provide any information about the changes within an issue. Therefore, this research is longitudinal to study the change and development in German Mittelstand-firms. Data from secondary sources, especially surveys, can be recombined to create new data sets. Thus, it is possible to conduct longitudinal research because data from a series of surveys asking the same question can be combined into a new data set (Saunders et al., 2019).

Data Collection and Data Analysis

The work investigates the trend of CSR engagement and, therefore, determines the relative changes (trend) over time using statistics. Index numbers are a suitable basis of comparison to the relative magnitude for each data value. The survey data delivers value measured in percentage terms, and index numbers are also applicable. The index number at *Period 1* is always 100 (Saunders et al., 2019). The following formula was used to calculate index numbers for each data value:

$$Index\ Number\ (Period\ X) = \frac{Data\ value\ (Period\ X)}{Data\ value\ (Period\ 1)} \times 100$$

However, the change in an index number time series from one period to another is expressed as a percentage of its value in the first period. This statistical method is called the percentage change (PC), representing the degree of change over time, and can be applied to any quantity that can be measured longitudinally. This change can be easily calculated as follows:

$$Percentage\ Change = Index\ Number\ (Period\ \ X) - Index\ Number\ (Period\ 1)$$

Therefore, the PC is appropriate to determine the change in CSR engagement. The PC can be calculated by synthesising the previous two formulas into one:

$$Percentage\ Change\ (Period\ X) = \frac{Data\ value\ (Period\ X) - Data\ value\ (Period\ 1)}{Data\ value\ (Period\ 1)} \times 100$$

Trend exploration requires a basic reference value. The formula represents this value as *Data value (Period 1).* The development of the key factors of CSR engagement was analysed starting from the year 2007 *(Period 1),* so the basic value refers to *Period 1.* To differentiate the Mittelstand-firms into size groups, the IfM Bonn (2020b) definition was used, leading to the following categories: small and medium-sized firms (< 500 employees) and large-sized firms (≥ 500 employees). Therefore, *Period 1* for small and medium-sized Mittelstand-firms refers to the data from Gilde GmbH (2007), and *Period 1* for large companies refers to Bertelsmann Stiftung (2007). The explanation for this choice is addressed in section *3.3*, which discusses the methodologies and methods of the secondary sources.

The development of each determining factor is based on the examination of its several sub-aspects. To ensure clarity and comprehension, line graphs, often applied when analysing trends, are not rational. Instead, multiple bar graphs illustrate the changes in every sub-aspect of a key factor in original percentages of the survey data (Saunders et al., 2019). The analysis consists, therefore, of the index number analysis and the PC analysis that follows from index numbers. The combination of PC analysis and original percentages of the survey data allows in figures delivers a thoughtful and understandable trend determination.

The key factors consist of several sub-aspects that were analysed and are listed in Table 3.

Key Factor	**Sub-aspects**
Awareness	➢ Very Important ➢ Important ➢ Less Important ➢ Not Important
Motivation/Goals	➢ Improvement of Reputation ➢ Motivation of Employees ➢ Increase of Economic Success ➢ Meeting Customers' Expectations ➢ Cost Reduction ➢ Ethical Motivation ➢ Environmental Motivation ➢ Securing Future Existence of Firm
Challenges	➢ Lack of Financial Resources ➢ Lack of Human Resources ➢ Insufficient Knowledge of CSR ➢ Lack of Interest from Stakeholders ➢ Doubts Concerning the Usefulness of CSR ➢ Lack of Time ➢ Rules and Policies
Activities	
Commitment to Employees	➢ Continuous Training ➢ Personalised Organisation of Working Hours ➢ Compatibility of Work and Family ➢ Additional Social Services and Securities ➢ Promotion of Health and Safety
Commitment to Society	➢ Promotion and Support of Social Initiatives ➢ Promotion and Support of Training Initiatives ➢ Promotion and Support of Cultural Initiatives ➢ Promotion and Support of Sport Initiatives ➢ Principles of Anti-Corruption

Commitment to Environment	➢ Reduction of Energy Consumption ➢ Measures for Sustainable Resource Use ➢ Recycling ➢ Environmentally Friendly Production Process ➢ Reduction of Emission ➢ Ecological Standard in Supply Chain ➢ Use of Renewable Energy
Communication	➢ Website and Internet ➢ Reports ➢ Marketing campaigns and Press ➢ Events and Internal Information

Table 3: Key factors and sub-aspects

3.2 Methodology and Methods of the Secondary Sources

For this book, the measurable concepts encapsulated by the conceptual framework are the key factors. This section discusses the methodology and methods used for data collection and data analysis adopted by the secondary sources. In addition, the section provides potential weaknesses of these sources that reflect the research scope and limitations, as well as its conclusions, which are based on secondary data. Thus, the main characteristics of the surveys Gilde GmbH (2007), Bertelsmann Stiftung (2007), EY (2012), and Pott et al. (2017) are presented.

Gilde GmbH (2007)
The first secondary data source was provided by Gilde GmbH (2007) and was produced on behalf of the EC. The aims were to investigate the extent to which CSR is widespread in small and medium-sized German Mittelstand enterprises and the nature of the expected development. Moreover, this study examined SMEs' goals and challenges of implementing CSR. Therefore, an online survey was answered by managers and owners of enterprises employing up to 500 people. This questionnaire was available on the website www.csr-mittelstand.de, in a link from the cooperation partners' newsletter, and was distributed by email with the help of the *Marktplatz Mittelstand* newsletter and *Wirtschaftsjunioren*. Of the 500 companies that responded between October and November 2006, 145 questionnaires were completed and suitable for further analysis. The questionnaire included questions on sector

and firm size, CSR activities, obstacles, motives, the role of stakeholders, and communication.

Bertelsmann Stiftung (2007)
This study focused on the social engagement of large Mittelstand-businesses in Germany. Therefore, the target group included enterprises with a minimum turnover of €50 million. The study investigated which CSR activities were planned and conducted, what influenced the conduct of social actions, and which motives were significant. The survey was distributed by post to owners and managers of 429 firms that met the outlined criteria in April 2007. The Department of Finance at the Business Institute at the University of Stuttgart on behalf of the *Bertelsmann Stiftung* and the *Stiftung Familienunternehmen* was responsible for survey distribution. This survey was conducted anonymously, and 103 companies replied; their answers were used for further analyses. The addressees required for the survey were determined from the database of the *Stiftung Familienunternehmen*, which lists many owner-managed Mittelstand-companies. Through the foundation, close contact with the businesses and their owners was possible. The foundation's personal approach to entrepreneurs and intensive support for all survey participants, for example, by a hotline and a cover letter to remind them of their participation, increased the response rate of this target group. Mittelstand-firms can consist of numerous sub-units or legal units. The owners, as well as the ownership structures of these businesses, are often difficult to determine for external actors. Thus, the study realised contact via the *Stiftung Familienunternehmen,* ensuring that the entrepreneurs were not contacted multiple times. The questionnaire contained questions on social engagement concerning the following topics: recipients and activities, extent and organisation, motivation, results, challenges, communication, and scale of the enterprise.

EY (2012)
This study was based on a systematic telephone survey of 500 randomly selected Mittelstand-companies in Germany. The study investigated the engagement of CSR in German Mittelstand-firms. The required information was provided by managing partners, managing directors, company spokespeople, and division heads (personnel, controlling, finance). The interviews were conducted in July 2011 by an opinion research institute on behalf of EY and the United Nations Educational, Scientific and Cultural Organization (UNESCO) Chair for Entrepreneurship and Intercultural Management. The questions were

thematically structured about the following key themes: CSR importance, activities, control mechanisms, responsibility, stakeholders, and communication.

Pott et al. (2017)
This study examined the status regarding Mittelstand-companies' CSR engagement and determined potential methods of improvement. The study was conducted by the Chair for International Accounting and Auditing at TU Dortmund University in cooperation with the consulting firm Baker Tilly. A questionnaire was sent to 4,917 companies; 229 companies participated. The online questionnaire was distributed between November and December 2016 and covered important aspects of CSR engagement. These include basic data about the enterprise, planning, organisation, implementation, motives, challenges, and CSR communication within the firms. The contact persons were mainly members of management. The main characteristics of the four surveys are summarised in Table 4.

	Gilde GmbH (2007)	**Bertelsmann Stiftung (2007)**	**EY (2012)**	**Pott et al. (2017)**
Methodological choice	Quantitative methodology			
Strategy	Survey distributed via internet/email	Survey distributed via post	Structured telephone survey	Survey distributed via internet/email
Year of data collection	2006	2007	2011	2016
Sample size	145	103	500	229
Number of employees	< 250: 94% 250-500: 6%	< 500: 21.5% 500-5000: 66.7% > 5000: 11.8%	≤ 115: 9% > 115: 91%	< 500: 49% 500-5000: 44% > 5000: 7%
Annual revenue in million €	No data	50-500: 77.5 % > 500: 22.5 %	No data	< 40: 20% 40-500: 63% > 500: 18%

Table 4: Characteristics of secondary sources

3.3 Suitability of Secondary Data

When using secondary data, there is the danger that these data may only partially meet the research needs (Saunders and Lewis, 2012). All secondary sources investigated the CSR engagement of Mittelstand-companies. However, the samples were slightly different, for instance, in the companies' targeted size, including number of employees and annual revenue, as Table 4 illustrates.

All four secondary sources chose the quantitative approach and the survey strategy. Moreover, these surveys were ad hoc, indicating that they did not collect data from an entire population. Instead, they were specific in their subject matter (Saunders and Lewis, 2012), focusing on the CSR activities of Mittelstand-companies, and were initiated by organisations and academic institutions. The use of questionnaires or structured interviews enables researchers to collect data and ensures that the same questions are asked in the same order. This structure helps researchers recombine and quantitatively analyse the new data sets. All studies employed the same methodological choice and strategy, making them comparable and suitable for further quantitative analysis. The secondary sources are based on a large representative sample. Compared to the other studies, Gilde GmbH (2007) examined small-to-medium Mittelstand-enterprises, evident from the number of employees (< 500), and thus did not provide data on annual revenue. In contrast, Bertelsmann Stiftung (2007) examined mostly large scale (> 500 employees) Mittelstand-firms. The EY (2012) source was chosen because the investigation time was in the middle of the relevant period (from the beginning of serious CSR interest in Germany until the newest available data). This source delivers data for the median time and adds information on the development of CSR in Mittelstand-companies. However, limitations lie within the vague determination of the employee number and the annual revenue that impede categorisation of the company's size class. This limitation can lead in further analyses to vagueness or deviation. Presumably, the investigated firms cover both small-to-medium and large Mittelstand-companies. Moreover, due to rounding in secondary sources, the percentages may not always appear to add up to 100 %. The latest study by Pott et al. (2017) was the most detailed concerning the number of questions and sub-aspects. This source's sample contains approximately half small-to-medium Mittelstand-companies and half larger enterprises. Thus, it is possible to make conclusions about the CSR engagement of Mittelstand-firms considering different company sizes in this study. The German Mittelstand includes different sizes of companies as long they fulfil the qualitative criteria outlined in the introduction. Therefore, the differentiation within the company size (small-to-medium and large Mittelstand-companies) adds value to this research. Thus, the datasets cover the relevant target group for the research. However, the newest available data is from 2017, so it was not possible to examine development in the last three years. Despite this limitation, the probability is high that the development from 2007 to 2017 is applicable to the time since 2018.

As outlined, the source of data is clear and was conducted and commissioned by widely known and reliable institutions in Germany. These institutions include foundations, like the *Bertelsmann Stiftung* and *Stiftung Familienunternehmen;* university facilities, such as the Department of Finance at the Business Institute at the University of Stuttgart and Chair for International Accounting and Auditing at TU Dortmund University; auditing/consulting companies, like EY and Baker Tilly; and other important institutions (i.e., the EC and the UNESCO Chair for Entrepreneurship and Intercultural Management). Thus, the data sources can be assessed as credible; the method of data collection, like the response rates, was described clearly.

The sources contain relevant data for the key factors that determine CSR engagement in Mittelstand-companies. However, the depth of questions for the factors differs, meaning not every source delivers an identical choice of sub-aspects in the factor analysis. For example, EY (2012) do not cover challenges but provide useful data for other factors. It is still possible to determine the development of CSR engagement and trends, even when a source is not able to offer information concerning every factor or sub-aspect. The use of four secondary sources delivers evidence for the development of CSR and makes the sources suitable for analysis. However, not all sub-aspects could be covered equally by the sources, which is a limitation.

The sources offered multiple-choice questions for the key factors to deepen understanding of CSR engagement. The answers were presented in bar graphs to illustrate the percentage occurrence of sub-aspects for every factor. Furthermore, the percentages were ranked from highest to lowest to present the importance of the sub-aspects. Large representative samples were collected, structured, and statistically analysed to illustrate the current situation of CSR engagement in the Mittelstand. However, the samples covered specific company sizes and not the full range of Mittelstand-companies. Thus, those results could be generalised concerning the investigated sample, but not for all

Mittelstand-firms. In contrast, the current study is divided into two size categories to allow for conclusions about differences in CSR engagement related to firm size. This approach enables the generalisation of the findings to the whole Mittelstand.

Overall, sections *3.1* and *3.2* proved the study's reliability because the data collection method and analysis procedures produce consistent findings. Moreover, validity is ensured due to the data collection methods accurately measuring what they intend to measure, and the research findings are about what they profess to be about in order to answer the research aim (Saunders and Lewis, 2012).

4. Results of the Data Analysis

4.1 Results

An index number analysis and PC analysis were conducted to determine the development of the key factors of the CSR engagement in German Mittelstand-companies from 2007 to 2017. The complete results are presented in the Appendices. The bar graphs in the following sections display the development of the key elements, given in the original percentages of the survey data, while the main results are presented for each factor for a better understanding. In the bar graphs, '2007 A' relates to the data from Gilde GmbH (2007), and '2007 B' to Bertelsmann Stiftung (2007). Thus, the main changes and trends in the engagement of Mittelstand-firms can be determined, while considering the differences within business size categories.

4.2 Awareness of CSR

Figure 6 presents the awareness of CSR in small-to-medium Mittelstand-firms. The sub-aspect 'Very Important' rose by 18% from 2007 to 2012 and by 26% by 2017; in 2012, 'Important' had gained 19% and, in 2017, 13%. Moreover, the PC analysis revealed the opposite development for the category 'Less important' (2017: PC = -38%). The category 'Not Important' (2012: PC = -71%; 2017: PC = -44%) decreased over time. Overall, the results of the PC analysis suggest, from 2007 to 2017, there is a clear trend of increasing awareness concerning CSR engagement in German Mittelstand-companies.

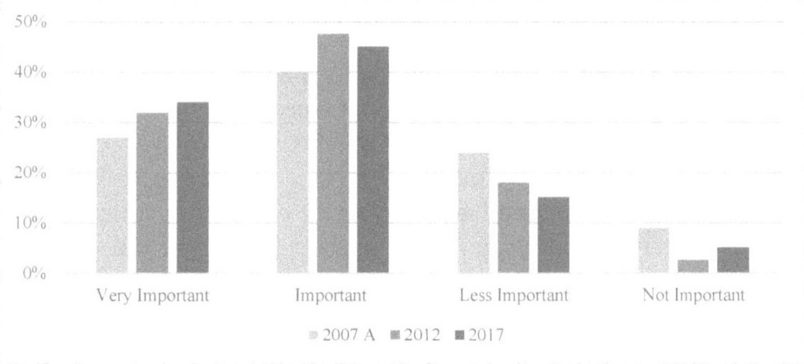

Figure 6: Awareness of CSR in small and medium-sized firms

4.3 Motivation and Goals of CSR Implementation

Figure 7 presents the development of CSR engagement in small-to-medium Mittelstand-firms, and Figure 8 addresses the same topic for large Mittelstand-companies. As Figure 7 illustrates, the PC analysis found four sub-aspects increased over ten years: 'Increase of Economic Success' (2017: PC = +9%), 'Meeting Customers' Expectations' (2017: PC = +11%), 'Cost Reduction' (2017: PC = +43%), and 'Ethical Motivation' (2017: PC = +35%). The PC analysis reveals that 'Motivation of Employees' remained nearly at the same level. 'Improvement of Reputation' and 'Motivation of Employees' are still the most important motivations/goals for small-to-medium Mittelstand-firms.

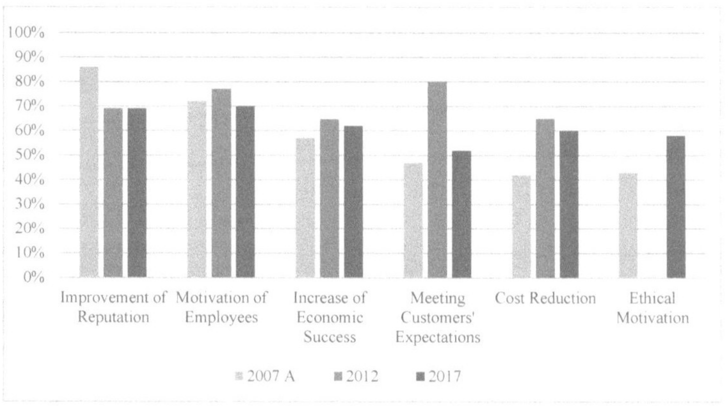

Figure 7: Motivation/goals of CSR implementation in small and medium-sized firms

In large Mittelstand-enterprises (Figure 8), the results from the PC analysis indicates that 'Increase of Economic Success' (2017: PC = +51%) and 'Cost Reduction' (2017: PC = +58%) became more important over time, similar to small-to-medium Mittelstand-enterprises. The additional sub-factor 'Securing Future Existence of the Firm' examined for this size category had a significant development (2012: PC = +77%; 2017: PC = +87%), making it the most important motivation. Similar to the small-to-medium firms, 'Improvement of Reputation' and 'Motivation of Employees' are, despite minor changes, the most motivating aspects. The category 'Meeting Customers' Expectations' had an undeterminable trend, and 'Environmental Motivation' stayed nearly at the same level. In contrast to small-to-medium firms, 'Ethical Motivation' dropped significantly (2017: PC = -29%).

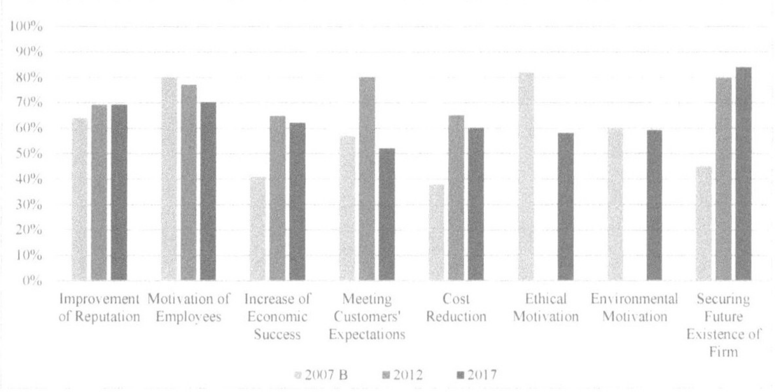

Figure 8: Motivation/goals of CSR implementation in large-sized firms

Overall, the analysis indicates that especially the economic-orientated motivations and goals, such as 'Motivation of Employees,' Improvement of Reputation', and 'Securing Future Existence of Firm', are the significant drivers of CSR engagement in all Mittelstand-firms.

4.4 Challenges of CSR Implementation

As Figure 9 displays, the small-to-medium businesses had a rapid decrease in four sub-aspects. From 2007 to 2017, the challenges 'Lack of Financial Resources' (2017: PC = -61%), 'Lack of Human Resources' (2017: PC = -35%), 'Insufficient Knowledge of CSR' (2017: PC = -55%), and 'Lack of Time' (2017: PC = -15%) became less influential to these enterprises. However, the challenges 'Lack of Interest from Stakeholders' (2017: PC = +26%) and 'Doubts Concerning the Usefulness of CSR' (2017: PC= +68%) increased, hindering these businesses' engagement in CSR. Based on the overall development of the challenges, 'Lack of Time' is the major challenging factor for small-to-medium Mittelstand-firms.

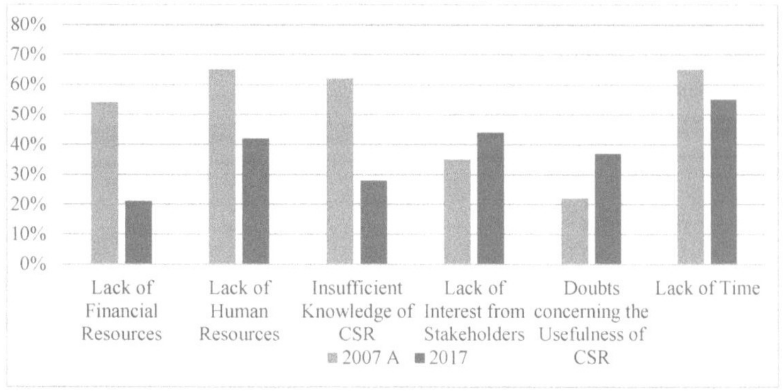

Figure 9: Challenges of CSR engagement in small and medium-sized firms

The PC analysis and Figure 10 reveal that the large Mittelstand-companies had a similar development in the sub-aspects 'Lack of Financial Resources' (2017: PC = -71%), 'Lack of Human Resources' (2017: PC = -16%), 'Insufficient Knowledge of CSR' (2017: PC = -13%), and 'Lack of Time' (2017: PC = -27%), as their negative impact on CSR engagement decreased. Moreover, the challenge related to 'Rules and Policies', especially relevant for large enterprises, decreased (2017: PC = -62%). Similar to the changes in small-to-medium firms, 'Lack of Interest from Stakeholders' (2017: PC= +52%) and 'Doubts Concerning the Usefulness of CSR' (2017: PC = +12%) rose. The analysis indicates that 'Lack of Time', 'Lack of Human Resources', and 'Lack of Interest from Stakeholders' are the main challenges for all Mittelstand-companies, hindering them from engaging in CSR.

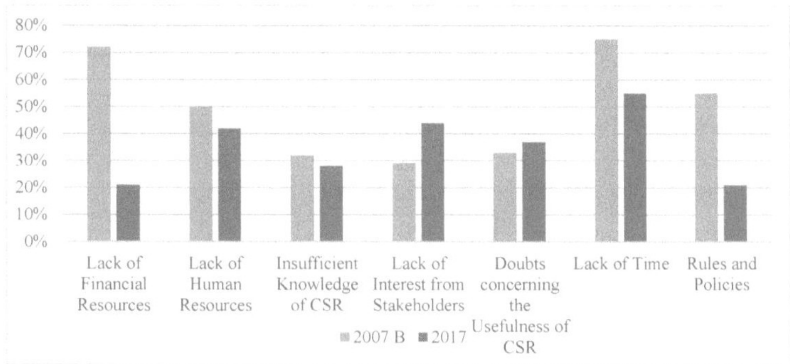

Figure 10: Challenges of CSR engagement in large-sized firms

4.5 CSR Activities

4.5.1 Commitment to Employees

This section presents the development of CSR activities in German Mittelstand-companies, particularly commitment to employees. As Figure 11 illustrates, the CSR activities in small-to-medium Mittelstand-enterprises with the strongest upward trend are 'Compatibility of Work and Family' (2017: PC = +93%) and 'Promotion of Health and Safety' (2017: PC = +47%). Notably, 'Continuous Training' and 'Personalised Organisation of Working Hours' have some variability, and conclusions on a clear upward or downward trend are not possible. However, these are still dominant activities concerning commitment to employees.

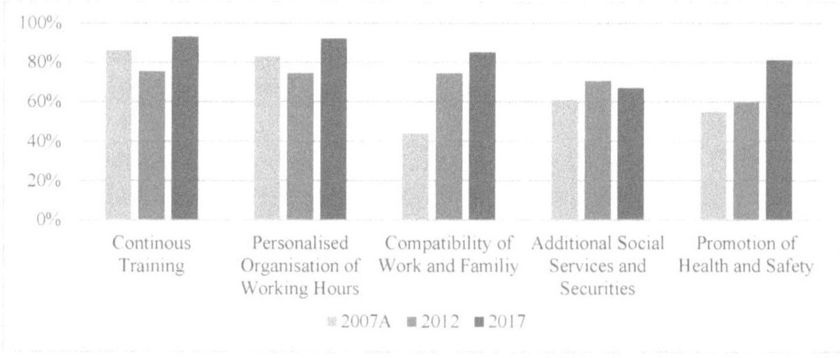

Figure 11: Commitment to employees in small and medium-sized firms

As Figure 12 illustrates and the PC analysis confirms, a similar development is observable in large Mittelstand-businesses: 'Compatibility of Work and Family' (2017: PC = +52%) and 'Promotion of Health and Safety' (2017: PC = +138%) have strong upward trends. Comparable to smaller businesses, 'Continuous Training' is the most frequently applied activity for employees in larger Mittelstand-firms. Overall, all Mittelstand-companies tend to strengthen their engagement for employees in the areas of training and work-life balance.

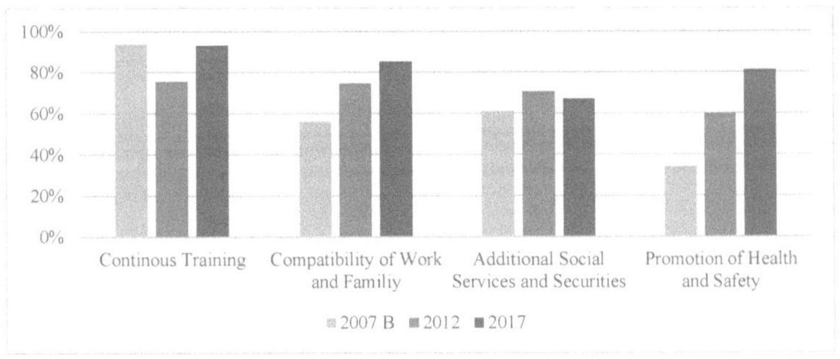

Figure 12: Commitment to employees in large-sized firms

4.5.2 Commitment to Society

Figure 13 and the PC analysis reveal 'Promotion and Support of Social Initiatives' in small-to-medium Mittelstand-firms rose (2017: PC = +18%), followed by 'Promotion and Support of Sport Initiatives' (2017: PC = +15%). Regarding the development in larger Mittelstand-firms (Figure 14), the activities 'Promotion and Support of Social Initiatives' (2017: PC = +17%) and 'Promotion and Support of Training Initiatives' (2017: PC = +69%) intensified between 2007 and 2017. However, some categories, like 'Promotion and Support of Social Initiatives', had some variation over the years without a clear trend, but their importance is still visible. The analysis of the commitment to society supports the findings from the previous section, indicating a positive development or strong CSR engagement in activities like 'Promotion and Support of Social Initiatives' and 'Promotion and Support of Training Initiatives' for all Mittelstand-firms.

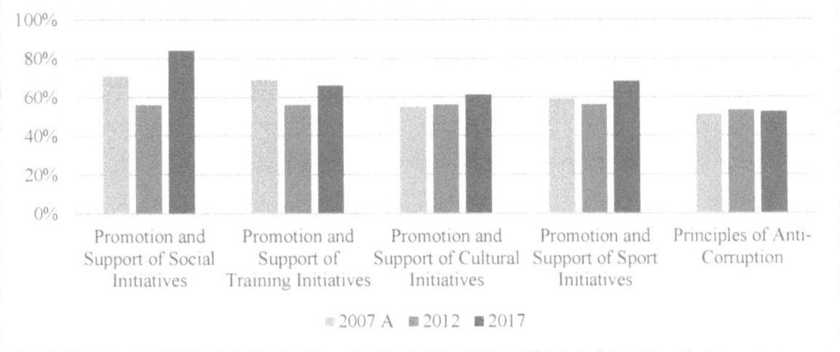

Figure 13: Commitment to society in small and medium-sized firms

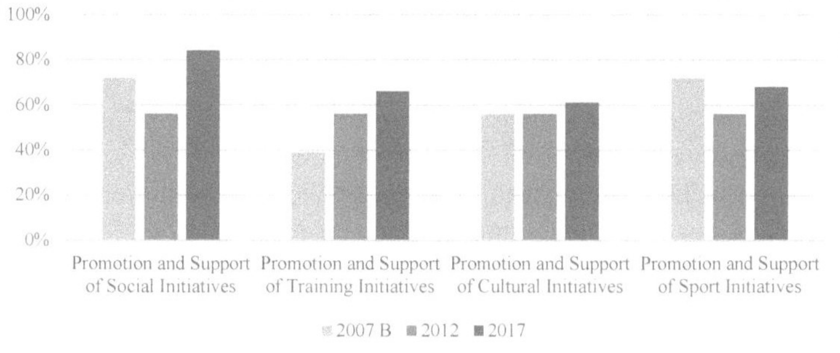

Figure 14: Commitment to society in large-sized firms

4.5.3 Commitment to Environment

Figure 15 displays the development of CSR engagement in original percentages of the survey data in small-to-medium Mittelstand-firms, and Figure 16 provides the same topic for large Mittelstand-companies. In small-to-medium Mittelstand-firms, the PC analysis indicates an upward trend for the following activities from 2007 to 2017: 'Reduction of Energy Consumption' (2017: PC = +18%), 'Measures for Sustainable Resource Use' (2017: PC = +22%), 'Recycling' (2017: PC = +19%), 'Reduction of Emission' (2017: PC = +25%), and 'Use of Renewable Energy' (2017: PC = +59%). For the other aspects, 'Environmentally Friendly Production Processes' has no clear trend, and the category 'Ecological Standard in Supply Chain' (2017: PC = -19%) tended to be applied less by firms over time.

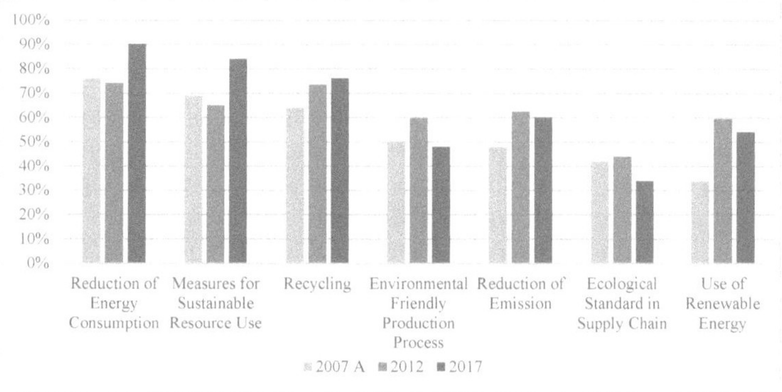

Figure 15: Commitment to environment in small and medium-sized firms

The PC analysis of the large Mittelstand-enterprises revealed (Figure 16) that 'Reduction of Energy Consumption' (2017: PC = +8%), 'Measures for Sustainable Resource Use' (2017: PC = +9%), and 'Reduction of Emission' (2017: PC = +6%) tend to be more frequently used. However, the relative changes for these activities compared to the small-to-medium Mittelstand-firms are smaller. Furthermore, 'Ecological Standard in Supply Chain' (2017: PC = -41%) and 'Recycling' (2017: PC = -4%) was applied less in these firms. Additionally, there is some variation in categories like 'Reduction of Energy Consumption' and 'Measures for Sustainable Resource Use', preventing conclusions about a clear upward or downward trend.

Overall, 'Reduction of Energy Consumption' and 'Measures for Sustainable Resource Use' are the most preferred activities for all Mittelstand-firms. They held the strongest positions among the environmental CSR engagement for ten years.

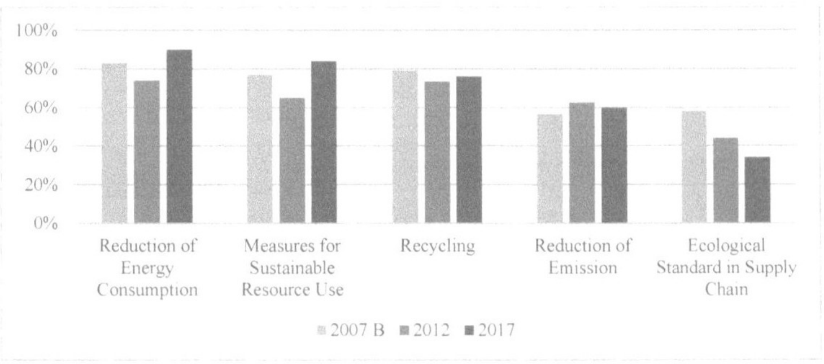

Figure 16: Commitment to environment in large-sized firms

4.6 Communication of CRS Engagement

This section presents the results related to the development of communication about CSR engagement in Mittelstand-firms. As Figure 17 and the PC analysis reveal, all communication activities gained significant importance for small-to-medium Mittelstand-firms. From 2007 to 2017, the utilisation of 'Website and Internet' (2017: PC = +113%), 'Reports' (2017: PC = +450%), 'Marketing Campaigns and Press' (2017: PC = +225%), and 'Events and Internal Information' (2017: PC = +183%) massively intensified.

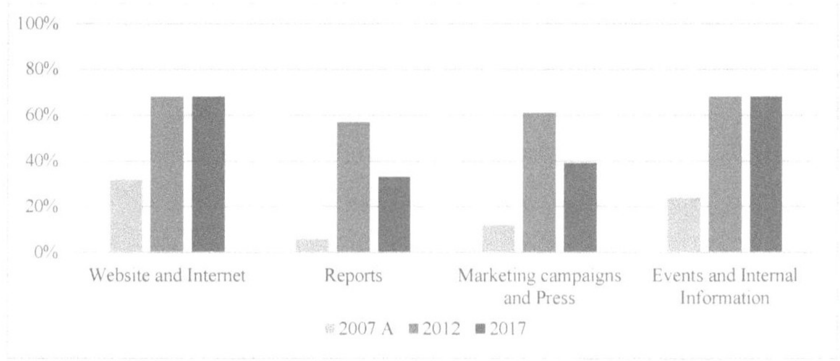

Figure 17: Communication of CSR engagement in small and medium-sized firms

A similar development happened in large Mittelstand enterprises (Figure 18): 'Website and Internet' (2017: PC = +258%) and 'Events and Internal Information' (2017: PC = +196%) were significantly more utilised. The ten-year change until 2017 demonstrates the importance of 'Reports' (2017: PC = -13%) and 'Marketing Campaigns and Press' (2017: PC = -9%) dropped slightly. However, the meaningfulness of these communication activities has some variation over the years. Overall, 'Website and Internet' and 'Events and Internal Information' were the most frequently utilised communication instruments in all Mittelstand-firms.

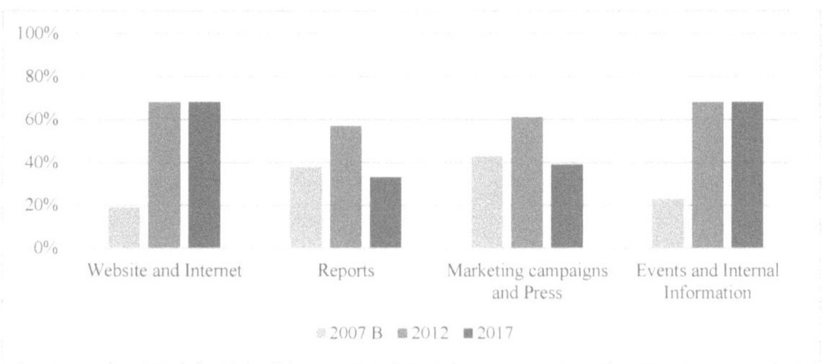

Figure 18: Communication of CSR engagement in large-sized firms

5. Interpretation of the Research Material

5.1 Awareness, Motivation and Goals of CSR Engagement

This study's data provides evidence that the awareness and importance of engaging in CSR among Mittelstand-companies increased. The positive development of the meaningfulness indicates a rising awareness due to the understanding that CSR management is compulsory for a company's long-term security, which was proven by the PC analysis investigating motivations and goals. According to Fassin (2008), without CSR, the long-term existence of a firm can be endangered, and operational risks are likely to appear. As mentioned in the literature review, a main characteristic of SMEs in comparison to larger enterprises is their close relationship to employees, making them the most important. This observation was also confirmed by studies ranking the meaningfulness of stakeholders in Mittelstand-firms (Gilde GmbH, 2007; EY, 2012). Consequently, employees are significant to Mittelstand-firms because they affect the success of these companies. As the study's results demonstrate, 'Motivation of Employees' is one of the major motivations to engage in CSR because the management of stakeholder relationships contributes to the achievement of economic objectives and wealth creation (Garriga and Melé, 2004). The results are in accordance with prior research on this specific issue (Mohnen, 2018). Mohnen (2018) has demonstrated that Mittelstand-firms achieve economic success through long-term orientation of their business policy by implementing measures for employee qualification and improvement of the working atmosphere. These activities can be perceived as short-term issues but are part of a long-term CSR approach.

Moreover, the results indicate that CSR is understood as an opportunity to realise strategic plans like meeting customer expectations and possibly gaining access to new markets. Ecological and social motivations as action drivers exist, but economic drivers have the dominant role (Maaß et al., 2014). Many companies confirmed that their expectations of their motives and goals were achieved with minor differences to their assumptions. However, it is undoubtedly difficult to objectively record economic success based on CSR activities because the impact happens indirectly and becomes notable with a time lag (Bertelsmann Stiftung, 2007; Pott et al., 2017).

Overall, the rising positive perception of CSR in Mittelstand-companies between 2007 and 2017 illustrates a win-win potential because many companies seem to exploit the potential advantages of CSR engagement. In addition to society and environment, the Mittelstand-company itself can benefit from CSR in the long run. An unsystematic implementation or even avoidance of CSR would prevent the company from enjoying the numerous advantages. Nevertheless, it is necessary to determine whether success control is based on subjective impressions or a systematic control mechanism.

5.2 Challenges of CSR Engagement

The current study found that lack of time, insufficient interest from stakeholders, and lack of staff were Mittelstand-companies' greatest challenges over time. These results correspond to the findings of previous works (Spence and Lozano, 2000; Perrini et al., 2007) stating that additional investment (time, finances, and energy) hinder companies from engaging in CSR, especially in smaller firms. This result may be explained by the fact that lack of time, personnel resources and insufficient knowledge of CSR are tightly connected and could be solved through consultation with experts in CSR (Pott et al., 2017).

Moreover, the lack of financial resources is relatively minor, and thus using external support is possible. An appropriate advisory could make recommendations for action regarding CSR activities based on a company's analysis. Consequently, external support could save time that the company would have invested in creating a CSR approach by itself and personnel resources by relocating responsibility for this issue to the advisory team (Pott et al., 2017). Therefore, the challenges stated by the Mittelstand-firms could be minimised. Another solution might be intensified cooperation with business partners to realise shared goals in CSR (Bertelsmann Stiftung, 2007). This solution would save time and exploit potentials in the social and environmental engagement of Mittelstand-firms.

The analysis demonstrated that most of the perceived challenges decreased in the examined period; however, the decrease of challenges for small-to-medium Mittelstand-firms was more intense than in large enterprises. This result is likely related to the fact that the initial CSR focus was on large firms, so their engagement was accompanied by earlier awareness and legal requirements (Kechiche and Soparnot, 2012). In contrast, the necessity for CSR implementation in smaller firms was recognised later, explaining the intensified need for action and the reduction of challenges. Moreover, the development of CSR engagement indicates that the recognition of the specific term 'CSR' might be the reason for increased awareness, although business responsibility for society and environment in German Mittelstand-companies has a long tradition (Gilde GmbH, 2007). Mittelstand-business owners' internal motivation to contribute to social welfare, especially for their own employees, is based on the conviction that this contribution produces an additional value (Heblich and Gold, 2008). On the one hand, this perception does not allow difficulties to hinder Mittelstand-companies' CSR engagement and problems potentially decrease over time. On the other hand, the owners' conception of CSR engagement is too subjective, allowing them to overlook challenges and neglect appropriate control mechanisms.

5.3 Activities

5.3.1 Employees

Regarding commitment to employees, the analysis proves that the creation of optimal working conditions is significant for Mittelstand-companies. These firms appreciate the value of well-trained and motivated staff. The development of CSR activities for employees is driven by the demographic change and thus by shortages in the skilled workforce (Kranzusch et al., 2017). Consequently, Mittelstand-companies are increasingly dependent on being attractive employers. These results confirm those of other studies (Heblich and Gold, 2008): the recruitment of potential employees contributing their expertise to the enterprises' success and the employed staff's motivation is essential for future performance. For long-term success, a company should offer not only monetary benefits but also non-monetary incentives and social benefits, for example, the creation of sports activities or company-owned childcare, to attract and retain employees. The criteria of work-life balance and a pleasant work atmosphere are distinctive features of Mittelstand-companies, unlike large companies where a better wage is often the attraction. Moreover, a company culture allowing employees to contribute, obtain information regarding the firm's development, and communicate openly can support firm trust and work ethic (Spence et al., 2003; Habisch, 2004; Murillo and Lozano, 2006).

Although the changes over time within this investigated aspect indicate a clear positive trend for employee training and work-life balance, the study did not find significant differences between the firms' size categories. However, the results are consistent with that of Icks et al.

(2015), who state that all measures that make employees feel connected to and identify with the company will undoubtedly help to create a positive working atmosphere and thus have a positive impact on company productivity.

5.3.2 Society

The current study found positive changes within social CSR engagement in Mittelstand-firms, particularly for training and social initiatives. The chosen social activities for society must be consistent with the Mittelstand-company goals confirmed by this study's results (employee motivation and training, reputation improvement, security in a firm's future existence). Therefore, a firm must prioritise activities and consider the available resources to realise its aims (Welge et al., 2017; Mitchell et al., 2011; Maaß, 2010). These findings may be somewhat limited because it is not possible to state how many activities a firm conducted. Consequently, despite the positive development, there is still potential for less engaged companies to widen their activities. The concentration on social activities within the core business facilitates the measurement of results.

5.3.3 Environment

Mittelstand-companies are already active concerning their environmental engagement. Considering the background of climate change and increasing scarcity of resources (Kranzusch et al., 2017), a strong ecological orientation of some companies using renewable energies, or a more focused reduction of CO2 emissions is desirable, despite the positive development indicated by the analysis. The implementation of employee training on energy-efficiency could also lead to further cost savings for Mittelstand-companies that do not yet offer such training courses. However, companies have already improved their attitudes toward environmentally friendly production and responsible use of resources. This environmental engagement also provides evidence that Mittelstand-companies' actions are orientated toward their economic goals (Maaß et al., 2014).

Surprisingly, the importance of suppliers addressed by the sub-factor 'Ecological Standards in Supply Chain' lost importance. This result is critical because a successful CSR (and sustainability) management is primarily determined by the type of procurement, especially by the systematic selection of suppliers. Baden et al. (2011) produced a similar finding stating that the burden of imposed procurement policies causes increased costs, bureaucracy, and frustration, thus reducing CSR engagement for this aspect. However, more customers expect companies to not only demonstrate compliance with relevant sustainability aspects but also pass this sustainability obligation to their suppliers (Baden et al., 2011). Increased attention lies on the whole product life cycle, and consequently, all processes in the value chain are noticed. In particular, the final product offered to the market reveals much about a company's attitude toward sustainability and environmental aspects. For an increasing number of consumers, this becomes the selection criteria and can affect the success of the Mittelstand-company (Baden et al., 2009). Therefore, the business must arrange appropriate purchasing management that can integrate and cope with environmental requirements and risks.

5.3.4 Summary

In general, Mittelstand-companies actively implement CSR activities for employees, society, and environment, and this engagement positively developed in most areas from 2007 to 2017. The analysis also revealed that, despite minor differences, the overall development of small-to-medium and large enterprises is similar. Based on the motivation and goals to implement CSR, the conducted activities also follow the dominant economic aims of Mittelstand-firms (Jenkins, 2006). Enterprises naturally aim to meet the existing preferences and wishes of their stakeholders (Maaß et al., 2014), which is especially evident in activities concerning employees. In addition, other activities indicate that the implemented activities have potentially high value for other stakeholders. The choice of CSR activities is not fortuitously, but instead strategically, analysed to increase the probability of satisfying stakeholder demands (Freeman, 2010).

The data analysis provides a direction for the development of CSR engagement; however, a note of caution is due since concrete answers to the company's basic characteristics cannot be determined. For example, stating how many activities a company conducted in a CSR area is not possible.

The present study raises the possibility that Mittelstand-companies with the potential to expand their CSR engagement should follow a planned, precisely defined implementation approach. Otherwise, it is likely that challenges like lack of time, human resources, or knowledge in the field of CSR will occur, although these difficulties are avoidable (Jonker et al., 2011). An unstructured establishment of a CSR strategy would reduce not only the possible positive effects on society and the environment but also weaken a Mittelstand-company's market position. Furthermore, customers could change their consumer behaviour and switch to companies that act socially and sustainably, so competitors would benefit from a more targeted CSR approach (Porter and Kramer, 2006).

Pott et al. (2017) found some potential weaknesses in the planning and organisation of CSR activities, which could hinder or diminish the long-term development of CSR efforts. For instance, observing nationwide production in Germany, they found CSR measures are often only conducted in the local environment, so not all stakeholder may be fully addressed. The responsibility for the organisation and implementation of CSR activities is often located exclusively inside the firm. Here, external help from consultants is desirable to create new impulses and ideas for the company's activities. Moreover, Pott et al. (2017) state that 23% of German SMEs do not implement CSR measures in their strategic planning, and only 28% of the companies provide an annual budget for CSR activities. There is clearly a significant potential for improvement in CSR integration as part of strategic planning to enable long-term success.

Mittelstand-firms' CSR engagement seems to be characterised by a specific mixture of responsibility and a clear purpose. The CSR activities are related to the companies' assets and resources and their area of influence. Mittelstand-companies arguably accept liability for their employees and their sphere of activity, thus securing the future existence of the firm (Bertelsmann Stiftung, 2007). In addition to being successful performers in the German economy, Mittelstand-companies create and stabilise new job offers (IfM Bonn, 2020d). This approach meets the demands of many people expecting responsible behaviour from companies regarding the labour market. Due to the high connection between CSR engagement and economic goals (Jenkins, 2006), company characteristics, like turnover, industry, and number of employees, have a vast influence on CSR engagement. This observation is an important issue for further research.

5.4 CSR Communication

Mittelstand-firms' CSR communication had the most drastic changes over time. According to Argenti and Druckenmiller (2004), companies apply corporate communication to align stakeholder's and firm's interests. In addition to the conducted CSR activities, communication about the engagement of a Mittelstand-firm can contribute to the success of CSR engagement. Using purposeful communication helps the firm inform the stakeholders about the enterprise's aspirations (Parker et al., 2015). Thus, the engagement is more likely to be appreciated, and the CSR actions can reach their full potential (CSR Europe and GRI, 2017). Furthermore, CSR communication interconnects the factors of the firm's CSR approach, intensifying engagement and gaining feedback on the conducted methods to improve the approach. When a Mittelstand-company is silent about its CSR efforts, the addressees of this engagement (employees, society, environment) will not recognise the positive effects to the desired extent. The firm loses opportunities that could lead to further advantages (Ellerup Nielsen and Thomsen, 2009).

The firm's website and internet were one of the most frequently used communication methods. Despite the high rating, it is imaginable that, in the digitalised world, more Mittelstand-enterprises could implement a homepage or provide relevant CRS information through their websites. This result is also consistent with that of Dincer and Dincer (2010), who found that the number of SMEs with CSR information is relatively low, and companies do not exploit the full potential of their websites. The apparent advantages are the relatively cheap installation expenditures and the opportunity to reach and communicate with a range of stakeholders. This installation is also applicable to the implementation of an intranet for employees, simplifying internal communication.

Regarding report usage, large Mittelstand-companies that participated in the surveys were obligated to reveal their financial reports as well as aspects of their environmental and social engagement. Small-to-medium Mittelstand-firms seem to understand the benefits of voluntarily utilising an additional method of communication, as the positive development of this sub-aspect has revealed. However, to publish an additional report, the enterprises must be aware of the required resources to produce this report. Considering the long-term impact of CSR and its communication, the realised potentials should outweigh the costs (Pott et al., 2017).

A CSR report can be used as an internal control tool. For the preparation of such reports, in-depth information about internal processes is required and must be collected in advance. Thus, these reports serve the management as a guide for future investments and projects. With the help of a CSR report, a firm can quickly identify weaknesses in CSR and determine which strengths can be further developed (CSR Europe and GRI, 2017). A CSR report can also be used as a guide and control instrument for a company.

Mittelstand-companies are often part of the supply chain of MNEs that are increasingly screening their suppliers CSR. Thus, they decide on follow-up orders or new orders based on the CSR information provided. Because of the new CSR guideline prescribing sustainability reporting for large companies in the public interest, the topic has gained attention (Pott et al., 2017). This fact might explain the different results of small-to-medium and large Mittelstand-firms. Mittelstand-companies, as a long-term part of the supply chain of large companies, also must follow up with relevant information. Comprehensive reporting and the disclosure of relevant CSR information will certainly help gain new business partners and contracts, as well as maintain old, successful relationships (Pott et al., 2017). In addition, Parker et al. (2015) found that reports provide a possibility to deal with topics of stakeholders' interest in a detailed manner. The use of reports makes the external perception of the firm more strategically structured, and thus the company would benefit more from its CSR commitment (CSR Europe and GRI, 2017).

Furthermore, Pott et al. (2017) explain that the expectations directed at SME companies should not be perceived as bothersome additional expenses; instead, the companies can create numerous potential benefits and financial advantages through their CSR activities and functioning reporting. At first glance, CSR investment may seem to waste financial resources, but SMEs clearly need to develop a long-term mindset. In addition to the numerous long-term advantages that CSR can offer, like increasing employee motivation, recruiting new talents, saving costs, and expanding the customer base, disregarding the responsible use of human and production resources can harm companies' competitiveness and weaken their market positions. A sophisticated CSR strategy has numerous advantages that, in the long-term, exceed the expenditure for CSR efforts.

Currently, different guidelines for CSR implementation exist for larger companies (EC, 2020). However, no specific publications guide or advise SMEs to engage in CSR or consider the characteristics of smaller enterprises. Such guidelines for CSR in SMEs would offer an orientation and conceptual framework, thereby saving firm resources for model development. Consequently, further research in this area would be highly beneficial for SMEs.

However, defining responsibility within a Mittelstand-company is vital to all areas of CSR. Here, the involvement of an external advisory should consider the firm's individual characteristics and resources. Considering the major challenges of CSR implementation, an exclusive internal responsibility approach does not seem purposeful. According to Pott et al. (2017), the companies rated the success of their CSR communication as partially satisfying. Addressing employees and customers reaches the firms' goals. However, communication with stakeholders, like potential customers located outside the direct sphere of influence, do not meet the expectations of the Mittelstand-firms (Pott et al., 2017). Therefore, appropriate planning, conduct, control mechanisms, and possibly external support are required to realise the initial CSR aims of a Mittelstand-firm.

Furthermore, Pott et al. (2017) found that most CSR activities are conducted in the local and regional area, reaching nearby stakeholders and supporting the social capital approach. However, this behaviour can also negatively influence the achievement of CSR goals and communication with farther locations. It is not clear which company size is particularly affected, but this finding should be deliberated in the process of CSR implementation. Depending on a firm's individual characteristics, the focus on local and regional networks is rational (Habisch, 2004; Murillo and Lozano, 2006). If circumstances allow, widening CSR engagement, maybe to a national area, should be deployed. Further investigations, which account for these variables, need to be undertaken.

6. Managerial Implications

The development of a Mittelstand-company's CSR-approach is determined by the changes within the key factors of CSR engagement (Conceptual framework). The work suggests that managers should conduct a thorough analysis of the firm considering the following aspects: firm size and locations, employees (number and structure), organisation (e.g., ownership), market positioning, social and political surroundings, financial assets, effects on the environment (e.g., production processes, supply chain, usage of energy), rules and policies, and other aspects. The company analysis enables managers to make the most appropriate choices for the CSR approach. In the next step, while establishing a strategy, the firm should pay attention to the company's philosophy, culture, leadership, stakeholder demands, risk considerations, and defined concrete goals. Furthermore, after defining the aims, an action plan that accounts for the available CSR budget, time horizon, and the evaluation and prioritisation of CSR activities is required. Next, during the plan's execution, the organisation of CSR activities, allocation of responsibility, consultation of CSR experts, CSR communication, and installation of control mechanisms (e.g., IT support, key performance indicators) is advisable. Reporting the conducted activities is tightly connected to the execution. The company should review the current reporting system and consider a specialised CSR reporting method. This method can be realised in various ways, for example, the annual report, specialised environmental or social reports, or CSR reports. Lastly, the evaluation of the previous steps in the CSR approach of a Mittelstand-firm should measure the results of the conducted activities, identify potentials and weaknesses, determine trends, and benchmark the CSR performance. Afterward, the firm can adjust its strategy and goals and repeat all steps. Regularly actualising the general analysis of the firm is also recommended because the CSR approach should be an integral part of the business strategy. Continuously undergoing this process results in a visible trend in the long-term. Practitioners and managers can use this study's results to facilitate the decision-making process and develop a structured approach for their CSR engagement. This process is visualised in the following Figure 19.

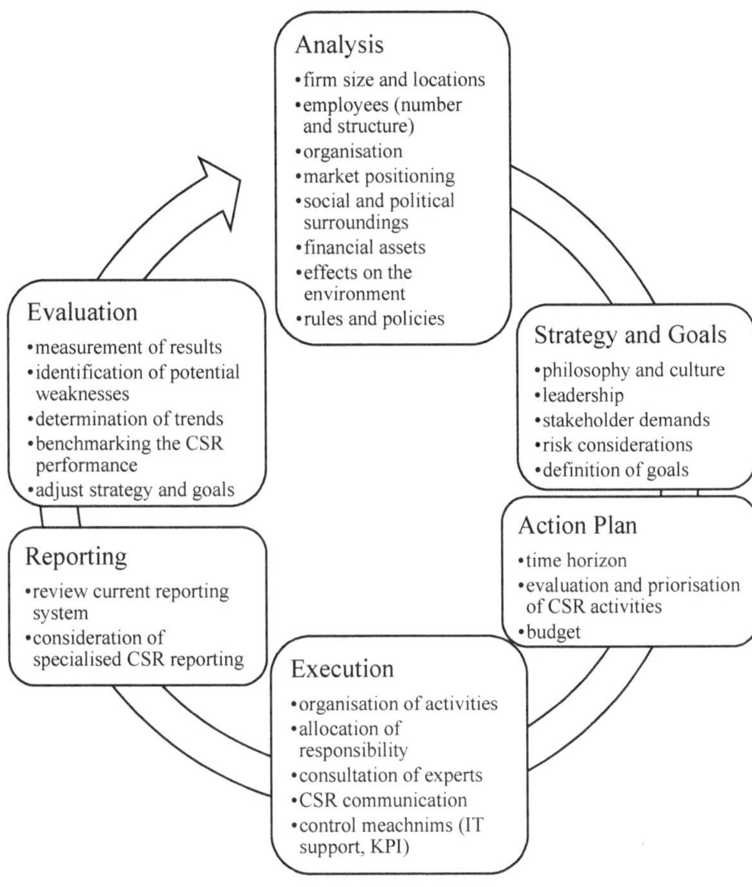

Figure 19: CSR cycle in SMEs

Source: Own illustration.

The following concepts relate to the outlined points in Figure 19, offering orientation for CSR implementation for management.

6.1 Approaches for Analysis and Strategy Development

When developing a strategic approach to CSR, a firm must consider its influence on society as well as society's effects on the company. If society offers a good government and reliable law, businesses can benefit through their own protection from exploitation. Furthermore, well-developed healthcare and education systems support the creation of a productive workforce, which firms require. Consequently, using these assets, businesses can offer jobs, provide innovation and wealth to society, and improve social conditions and living standards. Conversely, a poorly positioned firm offers lower wages and lost jobs and can negatively influence the community (Knudson, 2018). According to Porter and Cramer (2006), these connections are inside-out and outside-in linkages. Thus, a company with a goal to implement a CSR strategy must consider its outside-in linkages (social influences on competitiveness) and its inside-out linkages (mapping social impact of the value chain). Figure 20 depicts different aspects that a firm must recognise for its CSR strategy across its chain. A business should observe its value chain activities and pay attention to the positive and negative impacts that it possibly has on society and the environment.

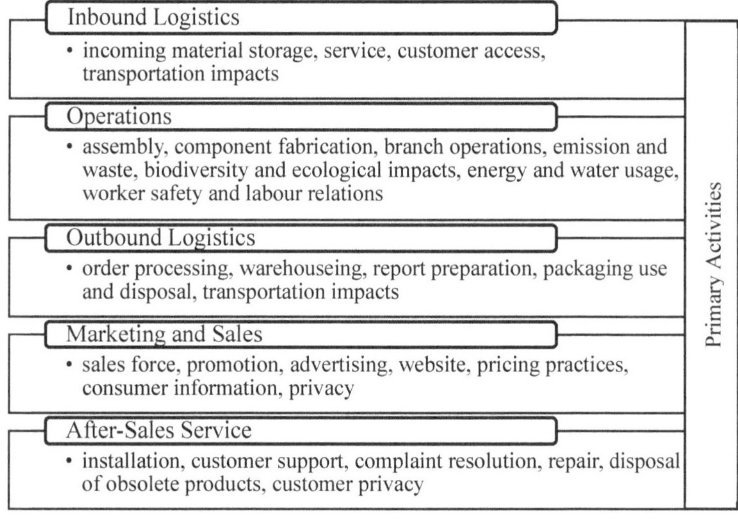

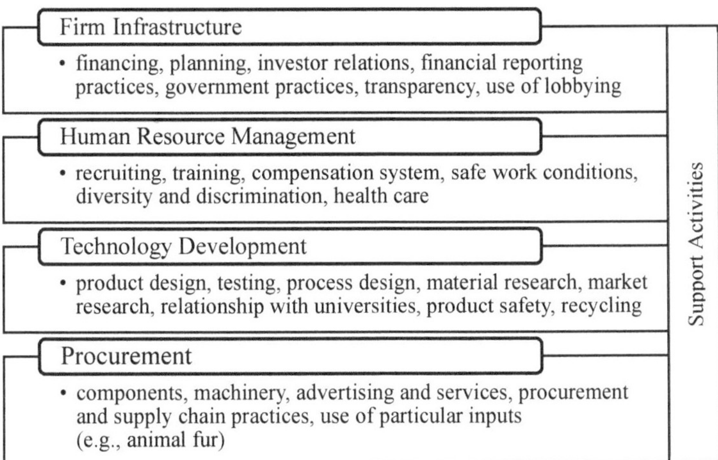

Figure 20: Inside-out linkages

Source: Adapted from Porter and Kramer (2006).

Effective CSR requires understanding the social dimensions of the firm's competitive environment. Here, the outside-in linkages refer to the company's ability to improve productivity and execute strategy. Therefore, Porter's diamond framework can be applied. This framework consists of four parts: context for strategy and rivalry, local demand conditions, related and supporting industries, and factor (input) conditions (Porter and Kramer, 2006). Figure 21 presents the outside-in linkages that a company should consider.

The mapping and consideration of inside-out and outside-in linkages enable a business to widen its view of its potential areas of influence, which may have an economic, environmental, or social nature. A sophisticated and strong CSR strategy can then support the creation of value in these areas (Knudson, 2018).

Moreover, certain positive characteristics of SMEs can help implement and realise their CSR approach. Although these characteristics were discussed in section *2.2*, and a short summary is provided to highlight the major facts (Jenkins, 2009):

- SMEs are flexible and adaptable, reacting quickly to changing circumstances; for instance, SMEs can take advantage of new niche markets.
- SMEs are often creative and innovative, which can be applied to the development of innovative CSR approaches.

- ➢ The owner-manager is closer to the organisation so can more easily influence the firm's values and culture.
- ➢ The communication in SMEs is fluid and open, allowing values to be implemented across the organisation and CSR information to spread quickly.

➢ Leaner and fewer hierarchical management structures support the involvement of all employees in CSR programmes (Jenkins, 2009).

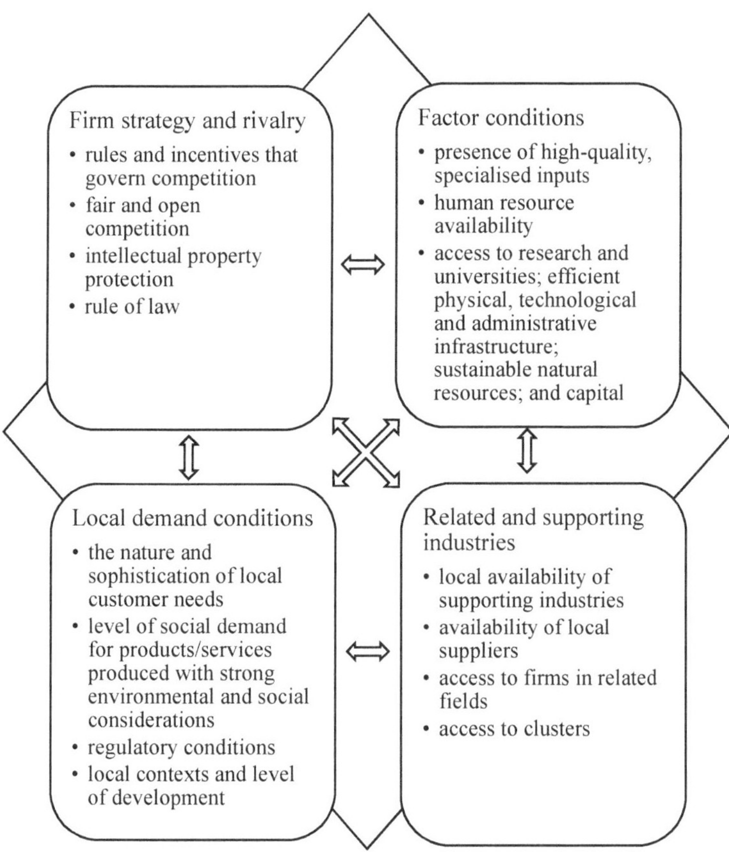

Figure 21: Outside-in linkages

Source: Adapted from Porter and Kramer (2006).

6.2 Benefits and Goals of the CSR Implementation

As mentioned, CSR can lead to various benefits for a company, which can act as a motivational factor or goal for businesses to engage in CSR. The benefits may be positive impacts on image and reputation, employee motivation and retention, cost savings, revenue and market share, and risk reduction (Weber, 2008). The potential benefits of CSR are discussed and summarised below to offer a useful overview of this topic.

The firm's image is its public's mental picture of the business, which is influenced by communicated messages. The firm's reputation is based on experiences and characteristics, including company stakeholders value judgement. Moreover, empirical research has demonstrated that CSR can influence reputation (Gray and Balmer, 1998). In the context of increasing society's sustainability concerns, the implementations of social and environmental aspects into the business model offers value to stakeholders and customers. Having a CSR strategy supports the firm's legitimacy and gains the trust of employees, customers, and investors (Smith, 2003). A firm's social performance has been proven to positively influence brand loyalty, increase employee interest in working for the company, and attract more investors due to reduced risks and long-term perspectives (Pivato et al., 2008; Carroll and Shabana, 2010). A company's legitimacy can strongly affect the firm's competitiveness, and therefore, a company should be willing to facilitate activities within the CSR strategy that support increased legitimacy. In addition, CSR communication and philanthropy may be part of these activities (Carroll and Shabana, 2010).

Businesses with well-developed CSR policies benefit from employee attraction, starting from a positive perception of the firm's reputation and image and including the desire for employment with a business with fair labour standards, appropriate wages, and incentives. Research has proven that CSR has a positive impact on employee engagement, commitment, performance, identification, and attitude toward the company (Aguinis & Glavas, 2012). Currently, CSR strategy is often tightly connected to human resource management, by developing and offering attractive employee incentives and benefits, for instance, childcare, job security, and training. This quality of working life is often a critical factor for employees during their job search. The CSR approach focusing on a fair and desirable work environment can even help to positively impact employee performance and prevent opposition from unsatisfied stakeholders (Kim et al., 2017; Knudson, 2018).

Additionally, CSR can lead to cost savings, which include time savings, efficiency gains, and better access to capital (Weber, 2008). The improvement of efficiency presupposes the analysis of utilised energy and material resources and the possibilities to reduce the costs and increase the environmental benefit. For example, the change from fossil-based to renewable energy enables a firm to reduce future costs. Furthermore, a switch to a new design packaging with a minimised resource use allows companies to save financial resources (Bocken et al., 2014). Savings also occur when companies communicate their CSR activities to different stakeholders that drive legal requirements and public opinion. The collaborative relationships with these groups enable the company to benefit from financial savings by avoiding fines due to unawareness of regulations or a reduced probability of lawsuits from wronged stakeholders (Weber, 2008). As a result of the global adoption of the 2030 Agenda for Sustainable Development, finance institutions and governments have recognised the need for more integration of sustainability strategies. Thus, the movement for more socially responsible investment intensified because companies with functioning CSR policies are more likely to attract investors focusing on sustainable firms and returns (Knudson, 2018).

Furthermore, CSR can benefit companies' sales and market shares (Weber, 2008). Due to the positive influence of rising legitimacy and reputation, employee and stakeholder satisfaction and customer loyalty can positively influence a firm's market position. For instance, businesses that produce under fair trade practices attract customers willing to pay more for this service or product because of nonmonetary aspects. Again, communication about these business practices is vital to raising awareness among customers (Knudson, 2018). Following this development, companies can offer products or services focused on environmental or social problems. Today, the necessity to overthink and adapt the consumption and production patterns is a growing concern for many customers. Companies addressing these issues could attract these customers' attention (Carroll & Shabana, 2010). The sales volume and the number of customers willing to pay more may increase when meeting customers' needs through stakeholder management and CSR (Knudson, 2018).

As addressed, CSR may help firms manage and reduce risks connected with negative environmental or social influences (Weber, 2008). Appropriate communication with stakeholders helps businesses to comprehend needs and regulations and reduce risks of offending social boundaries. Thus, clearly defining environmental and social values in a firm's CSR strategy is advisable, so the firm has orientation points for its performance. Moreover, management systems measuring performance may offer the latest data on CSR activities, indicate problems, and prevent crises. In the long-term, this approach enables companies to systematically manage and reduce risk (Knudson, 2018).

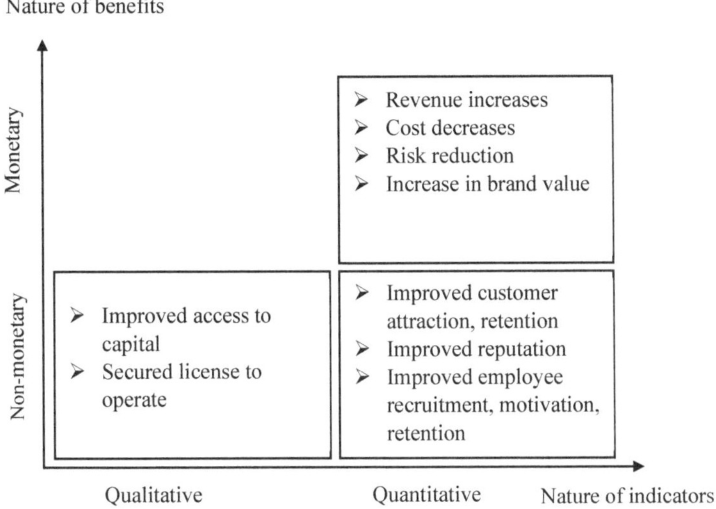

Figure 22: Business benefits from CSR

Source: Adapted from Weber (2008).

Weber (2008) provided an impact model mapping the presented benefits of CSR. Figure 22 illustrates that monetary and non-monetary benefits can lead to competitive value for a business. Revenue increases and cost decreases are monetary impacts and, for example, improved customer attraction and employee recruitment may be allocated to the non-monetary benefits. Moreover, these benefits can be differentiated by measurement methods (qualitative or quantitative). This division can help during the communication of CSR where firms must measure and monitor their activities using qualitative and quantitative indicators. The scope and combination of different CSR benefits advances the level of competitive advantage for a firm and contributes to its economic success (Knudson, 2018).

6.3 Possible Model for CSR Implementation in SMEs

Jenkins (2009) proposes a 'business opportunity' model of CSR for SMEs, arguing that it is important for SMEs to have an integrated and step-by-step approach to succeed with CSR policies. Therefore, it is necessary to recognise the unique characteristics of SMEs to capitalise on the 'business opportunity' offered to firms through the application of CSR. This model is presented in Figure 23 and consists of five steps.

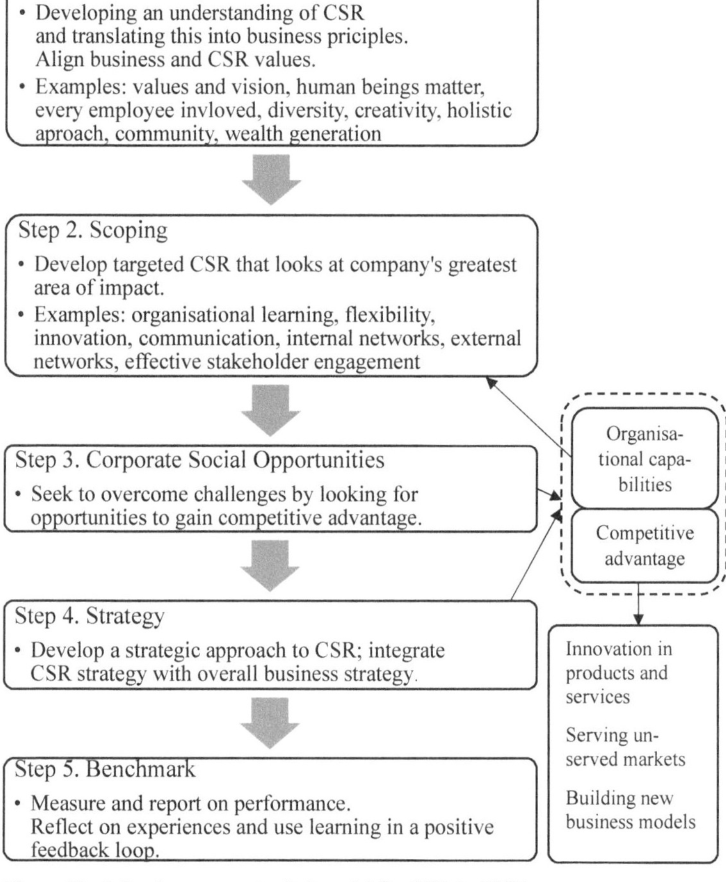

Figure 23: A 'business opportunity' model for CSR in SMEs

Source: Adapted from Jenkins (2009).

In Step 1, the SME needs to develop an understanding of CSR and transfer this into its own business principles. This step requires the active participation of the firm's owner and/or manager to build the values and principles that can incorporate different dimensions of CSR (e.g., social, environmental) (Jenkins, 2009). Here, the SME could orientate on the ten principles outlined by the United Nations Global Compact addressing social responsibilities toward employees, stakeholders, and future generations (Knudson, 2018). Table 5 depicts these ten principles. Furthermore, Jenkins (2009) proposes the following values a SME could consider: values and vision, human beings matter, every employee involved, diversity, creativity, holistic approach, community, and wealth generation.

Category	Principle
Human Rights	➢ Businesses should support and respect the protection of internationally proclaimed human rights ➢ Businesses should ensure that they are not complicit in human rights abuses
Labour	➢ Businesses should uphold the freedom of association and the effective recognition of the right to collective bargaining ➢ Businesses should eliminate all forms of forced and compulsory labour ➢ Businesses should support the effective abolition of child labour ➢ Businesses should eliminate discrimination in respect of employment and occupation
Environment	➢ Businesses should support a precautionary approach to environmental challenges ➢ Businesses should undertake initiatives to promote greater environmental responsibility ➢ Businesses should encourage the development and diffusion of environmentally friendly technologies
Anti-Corruption	➢ Businesses should work against corruption in all its forms, including extortion and bribery

Table 5: Ten UN Global Compact Principles

Source: Adapted from UN Global Compact (2020).

Step 2 embodies SMEs' searching for the most important values and dimensions of CSR relevant to their impact and operations. In particular, engagement with stakeholders is vital to understanding which aspects of CSR are key to a firm. Moreover, Knudson (2018) suggests that SMEs can consider the UN Sustainable Development Goals, which provide a set of proposed values. Through this resolution, the Member States of the United Nations aim to end all forms of poverty, tackle climate change, and fight inequalities (UN, 2020). Using these goals as guidance, SMEs can choose the most relevant goals for their business and utilise them as part of their CSR strategy. Table 6 provides an overview of the Sustainable Development Goals.

Dimension	Goal
Economical	➢ Decent work and economic growth ➢ Industry, innovation, and infrastructure ➢ Responsible consumption and production ➢ Reduced inequalities
Social	➢ No poverty ➢ Zero hunger ➢ Good health and well-being ➢ Quality education ➢ Sustainable cities and communities ➢ Gender equality ➢ Affordable and clean energy ➢ Peace, justice, and strong institutions
Environmental	➢ Clean water and sanitation ➢ Climate action ➢ Life below water ➢ Life on land

Table 6: UN Sustainable Development Goals

Source: Adapted from UN (2020).

Step 3 addresses the values and dimensions selected in the previous step, directing the opportunities and competitive advantages the company may gain. This step is closely related to the specific capabilities of SMEs and their ability to flexibly and innovatively address important social and environmental conditions.

Further, step 4 is concerned with the integration of CSR into the business strategy. Both step 3 and 4 rely on the application of organisational capabilities and can result in competitive advantages that can influence innovation in products and services, serving unserved markets, and building new business models.

Step 5 addresses the need for SMEs to measure and report their performance in order to learn and steadily improve (Jenkins, 2009). Knudson (2018) claims that, especially in steps 2 through 4, a firm should analyse its influence on society and society's impact upon it. In addition, the presented outside-in and inside-out linkages (Figures 20 and 21) could be useful when guiding a company's attention to strategic CSR aspects.

6.4 Orientation for CSR Communication and Reporting

Due to the increasing relevance of CSR reporting in SMEs, the GRI has also recognised the trend and developed a brochure with guidelines for reporting social, environmental, and economic topics, including practical guides for SMEs (GRI, 2014). Furthermore, the Bundesverband der Deutschen Industrie e.V. (BDI) published guidance for SMEs based on the G4-guidelines of GRI. These guidelines are organised as a checklist and include the steps presented in Table 7 (BDI, 2014).

Step	Activities
Step 1 Preparation	➢ Organising a team and distributing responsibility ➢ Creating a schedule/action plan and securing resources ➢ Developing a common understanding and defining relevant topics that the company is going to report on
Step 2 Connection	➢ Identifying the company's most important stakeholders and issues
Step 3 Data Collection	➢ Selecting appropriate performance indicators ➢ Collecting and analysing relevant information for the report, for example, questionnaires, interviews, IT-management systems
Step 4 Definition	➢ Deriving specific goals and measures from the analysis ➢ Linking the report closely to the firm's CSR strategy
Step 5 Report	➢ Finalising the report, which should be written in a comprehensible, clear and target group-oriented manner ➢ Distributing the report to the firm's stakeholders

Table 7: Reporting steps

Source: Adapted from BDI (2014).

The guidelines provide useful initial assistance for SMEs implementing CSR or sustainability reporting or aiming to improve existing reporting standards. More detailed information is provided in the current GRI standards. Additionally, SMEs in Germany can use other codices or guidelines for their CSR reporting (BDI, 2014). These guidelines include the United Nations Global Compact, The Sustainability Code (Deutscher Nachhaltigkeitskodex), Guidelines of Global Compact, OECD Guidelines, Carbon Disclosure Project, European Federation Financial Analysts Societies, Governance Kodex für Familienunternehmen, and the International Integrates Reporting Council (Pott et al., 2017; BDI, 2014). According to Pott et al. (2017), the most frequently used reporting guidelines in German SMEs are either self-designed or based on the GRI, the Sustainability Code, and the Governance Kodex für Familienunternehmen.

7. Conclusion

7.1 Main Findings of the Study

The purpose of the work was to determine the development of key factors affecting CSR engagement in German Mittelstand-companies. Differentiation into two size categories (small-to-medium and large) was conducted considering the heterogeneity of these firms.

The book indicates that CSR engagement from 2007 to 2017 intensified, which is reflected by the changes in the key elements. The in-depth analysis revealed the trend using index numbers and percentage change and provides evidence that awareness and importance of CSR have risen. The analysis demonstrates that securing the future existence of the firm, the motivation of employees, and the improvement of reputation tend to be the leading goals for CSR engagement in Mittelstand-firms. Although during the investigated period, several challenges became less influential, lack of time, human resources, and interest from stakeholders were the most hindering factors. Moreover, CSR activities concerning employees, society, and environment became, in general, more frequently applied. Some of the most significant activities are related to training, support of work-life balance, and reduction of energy consumption. Furthermore, different communication instruments addressing internal and external stakeholders gained importance.

The results highlight the often owner-managed Mittelstand-enterprises' focus on the achievement of economic aims in combination with a value-driven approach. This approach is especially visible in the positive trend for all key elements concerning the firms' employees. This study suggests that employees are the most critical stakeholders of Mittelstand-firms. Thus, this new understanding correlates with the stakeholder theory, which states that stakeholder relationship management aims to achieve economic goals (Garriga and Melé, 2004) primarily to secure the existence of the firms. Simultaneously, the results confirm the relevance of the social capital approach: the focus on the social, particularly employee wellbeing, confirms the Mittelstand-companies' appreciation of networks, norms, and trust intended to encourage participants and enforce common aims (Putnam, 1995).

Despite minor distinctions in the development of some sub-aspects, small-to-medium and large Mittelstand-firms were not significantly different. Reasons for the differences can be traced to the earlier necessity of large companies to implement CSR. However, the evidence from this study suggests that, over time, small-to-medium Mittelstand-firms will reach the confidence of action and required expertise for structured CSR implementation similar to large enterprises. To achieve better results in CSR implementation, Mittelstand-companies would highly benefit from expert consultation. This approach would minimise existing challenges and allow the companies to create a systematic CSR approach suitable for their businesses. Here, the results of the current study provide significant trends that can serve as a guide for Mittelstand-firms aiming to engage in CSR.

This work contributes to the increasingly important field of CSR in the SME context, investigating the German-Mittelstand as a major actor in the German economy. Moreover, the present study is the only investigation determining the changes and trends within the development of CSR engagement over time. As demanded by the academic literature, the provided quantitative analysis, based on large-scale samples, makes it possible to generalise the results. These key results provide some insights for both researchers and managers.

7.2 Limitations and Suggestions for Further Research

In this work, some limitations exist and have been addressed in the previous chapters. The main limitation is the differences in the investigated samples, which might have caused some vagueness or deviation. Although all secondary sources investigated the CSR engagement in Mittelstand-companies, the key factors were unequally addressed. Therefore, the analysis has some gaps, but the trends are still determinable. Furthermore, providing the exact number of conducted activities regarding the companies' size classes would have added a deeper understanding of the execution of CSR activities; however, this information was not obtainable. The last weakness is that the newest available data was from 2017, preventing investigation into developments in 2018, 2019, and 2020. However, the trends identified from 2007 to 2017 are likely applicable for the following years and present time.

Due to the high importance of economic goals that may have a vast influence on CSR engagement, considerable work is required to explore the interconnection between companies' characteristics (e.g., turnover and industry) and CSR implementation. In addition to communication, broader research is needed to examine success control mechanisms enabling a Mittelstand-firm to analyse and improve its future CSR engagement. Moreover, investigating the correlation between company size and the achievement of CSR communication goals toward stakeholders is of interest. Here, the stakeholder theory and the social capital model should be considered, including the area of influence of the CSR activities. Further, the influence of digitalisation should be considered during the implementation process of CSR. Digitalisation offers a wide range of opportunities for companies, but also involves certain challenges that need to be managed. Lastly, it is advisable to develop guidelines for CSR implementation in SMEs that would be especially beneficial for practitioners.

References

Abel-Koch, J. (2017) *Weltweit machen sich Mittelständler für gesellschaftliche Interessen stark.* Unknown place of publication: KfW Research. [Online] [Accessed on 7th April 2020] https://www.kfw.de/PDF/Download-Center/Konzernthemen/Research/PDF-Dokumente-Fokus-Volkswirtschaft/Fokus-Nr.-159-Januar-2017-CSR-im-Mittelstand.pdf

Ackerman, R.W. (1975) *The social challenge to business.* Harvard University Press, Cambridge, MA.

Aguinis, H. and Glavas, A. (2012) 'What we know and don't know about corporate social responsibility: A review and research agenda.' *Journal of Management*, 38(4), pp. 932-968.

Argenti, P.A., and Druckenmiller, B. (2004) 'Reputation and the corporate brand.' *Corporate Reputation Review*, 6(4) pp. 368-374.

Austin, J., Stevenson, H. and Wei-Skillern, J. (2006) 'Social and commercial entrepreneurship: same, different, or both?' *Entrepreneurship Theory and Practice*, 30(1), pp. 1-22.

Bundesministerium für Arbeit und Soziales. (2020) *CSR-Politik in Deutschland.* [Online] [Accessed on 21st April 2020] https://www.csr-in-deutschland.de/DE/Politik/CSR-national/csr-national.html

Baden, D., Harwood, I.A, Woodward, D.G. (2009) 'The effect of buyer pressure on suppliers in SMEs to demonstrate CSR practices: An added incentive or counterproductive?' *European Management Journal,* 27(6) pp. 429-441.

Baden, D., Harwood, I.A., Woodward, D.G. (2011) 'The effects of procurement policies on 'downstream' corporate social responsibility activity: Content-analytic insights into the views and actions of SME owner-managers.' *International Small Business Journal*, 29(3) pp. 259-277.

Barnett, A. (1997) 'Towards a stakeholder democracy'. *In* Kelly, G., Kelly, D. and Gamble, A. (eds.) *Stakeholder Capitalism.* Basingstoke: Macmillan, pp. 82–95.

BDI. (2014) In 7 Schritten zum Nachhaltigkeitsbericht: Ein praxisorientierter Leitfaden für mittelständische Unternehmen in Anlehnung an die G4-Leitlinien der Global Reporting Initiative (GRI). Berlin: BDI. [Online] [Accessed on 7th January 2021] https://bdi.eu/publikation/news/in-7-schritten-zum-nachhaltigkeitsbericht/

Besser, T. and Miller, N. (2001) 'Is the Good Corporation Dead? The Community Social Responsibility of Small Business', *Journal of Socio-economics*, 30(3) pp. 221-230.

Bertelsmann Stiftung. (2007) *Das Gesellschaftliche Engagement von Familienunternehmen. Dokumentation der Ergebnisse einer*

Unternehmensbefragung. Gütersloh: Bertelsmann Stiftung [Online] [Accessed on 21st April 2020] https://www.google.com/url?sa=t&rct=j&q=&esrc=s&source=web&cd=2&cad=rja&uact=8&ved=2ahUKEwiD4drkg_roAhUOilwKHRS1CmQQFjABegQIBBAB&url=https%3A%2F%2Fwww.familienunternehmen.de%2Fmedia%2Fpublic%2Fpdf%2Fpublikationen-studien%2Fstudien%2FStudie_Stiftung_Familienunternehmen_Das-Gesellschaftliche-Engagement-von-Familienunternehmen.pdf&usg=AOvVaw2bi-IBUZQTWBJZFq4uWX53

Bocken, N.M.P, Short, S.W., Rana, P. and Evans, S. (2014) 'A literature and practice review to develop sustainable business model archetypes.' *Journal of Cleaner Production*, 65 pp. 42-56.

Bos-Brouwers, H.E.J. (2010) 'Corporate Sustainability and Innovation in SMEs: Evidence of Themes and Activities in Practice.' *Business Strategy and the Environment,* 19(7) pp. 417-435.

Buschhausen, B. (2016) *Trau, schau, wem! Unternehmen in Deutschland.* Gütersloh: Bertelsmann Stiftung. [Online] [Accessed on 7th April 2020] https://www.google.com/ url?sa=t&rct=j&q=&esrc=s&source=web&cd=1&cad=rja&uact=8&ved=2ahUKEwiH79Tf4NjoAhVlolwKHQ3fCdAQFjAAegQIAxAB&url=https%3A%2F%2Fwww.bertelsmann-stiftung.de%2Ffileadmin%2Ffiles%2FBSt%2FPublikationen%2FGrauePublikationen%2FStudie__BS_Trau__schau__wem._Unternehmen_in_Deutschland_2016.pdf&usg=AOvVaw2CS1MeB19O8_D4fWLzAxHj

Carroll, A.B. (1979) 'A three-dimensional conceptual model of corporate social performance.' *Academy of Management Review*, 4(4) pp. 497-505.

Carroll, A.B. (1991) 'The Pyramid of Corporate Social Responsibility: Toward the Moral Management of Organizational Stakeholders.' *Business Horizons*, 34(4) pp. 39-48.

Carroll, A.B. (2016) 'Carroll's pyramid of CSR: taking another look.' *International Journal of Corporate Social Responsibility.* 1(1) pp. 1-8.

Carroll, A.B. and Brown, J.A. (2018) 'Corporate Social Responsibility: A Review of Current Concepts, Research, and Issues.' *In* Weber, J and Wasielewski, D. (eds.) *Corporate Social Responsibility.* U.K: Emerald Publishing Co., pp. 39-69.

Carroll, A.B. and Shabana, K.M. (2010) 'The business case for corporate social responsibility: A review of concepts, research and practice.' *International Journal of Management Reviews*, 12(1) pp. 85-105.

Castka, P., Balzarova, M., Bamber, C., Sharp, J. (2004) 'How Can SMEs Effectively Implement the CSR Agenda? A UK Case Study Perspective.' *Corporate Social Responsibility and Environmental Management*, 11(3) pp. 140-149.

Choi, J. and Wang, H. (2009) 'Stakeholder relations and the persistence of corporate financial performance.' *Strategic Management Journal*, 30(8) pp. 895-907.

CSR Europe and GRI. (2017) *Member State Implementation of Directive 2014/95/EU.* Unknown place of publication: CSR Europe and GRI. [Online] [Accessed on 7th April 2020] https://www.accountancyeurope.eu/wp-content/uploads/1711-NFRpublication-GRI-CSR-Europe.pdf

Davies, I. and Crane, A. (2010) 'Corporate social responsibility in small and medium-size enterprises: investigating employee engagement in fair trade companies.' *Business Ethics* 19(2) pp. 126-139.

Dincer, C. and Dincer, B. (2010) 'An investigation of Turkish small and medium-sized enterprises online CSR communication.' *Social Responsibility Journal*, 6(2) pp. 197-207.

Donaldson, T. and Preston, L.E. (1995) 'The stakeholder theory of the corporation: Concepts, evidence, & implications.' *Academy of Management Review*, 20(1), pp. 65-91.

Ellerup Nielsen, A. and Thomsen, C. (2009) 'CSR communication in small and medium-sized enterprises: A study of the attitudes and beliefs of middle managers.' *Corporate Communications: An International Journal*, 14(2) pp. 176-189.

Elkington, J. (1997) *Cannibals with forks: The triple bottom line of 21st century business*. Oxford: Capstone.

Ernst & Young GmbH. (2012) *Nachhaltige Unternehmensführung. Lage und aktuelle Entwicklungen im Mittelstand.* Essen: Ernst & Young GmbH. [Accessed on 21st April 2020] https://docplayer.org/57413318-Nachhaltige-unternehmensfuehrung.html

European Commission. (2011) *Communication From The Commission To The European Parliament, The Council, The European Economic And Social Committee And The Committee Of The Regions: A renewed EU strategy 2011-14 for Corporate Social Responsibility.* Brussels: European Commission. [Online] [Accessed on 7th April 2020] https://op.europa.eu/en/publication-detail/-/publication/ae5ada03-0dc3-48f8-9a32-0460e65ba7ed/language-en

European Commission. (2015) *Opportunity and Responsibility: How to help more small businesses to integrate social and environmental issues into what they do.* Unknown place of publication: European Commission. [Online] [Accessed on 7th April 2020] https://www.google.com/url?sa=t&rct=j&q=&esrc=s&source=web&cd=2&ved=2ahUKEwjUoczo2djoAhUEUcAKHTSFBOkQFjABegQIAxAB&url=http%3A%2F%2Fec.europa.eu%2FDocsRoom%2Fdocuments%2F11866%2Fattachm

ents%2F1%2Ftranslations%2Fen%2Frenditions%2Fpdf&usg=AOvVaw1aLadsXad7Y5HcseZZ6fiu

European Commission. (2020) *Corporate Social Responsibility & Responsible Business Conduct.* European Commission. [Online] [Accessed on 25th June 2020] https://ec.europa.eu/growth/industry/sustainability/corporate-social-responsibility_en

Fassin, Y. (2008) 'SMEs and the fallacy of formalizing CSR.' *Business Ethics: A European Review*, 17(4) pp. 364-378.

Fassin, Y., Van Rossem, A. Buelens, M. (2011) 'Small-business owner-managers' perceptions of business ethics and CSR-related concepts.' *Journal of Business Ethics*, 98(3) pp. 425-453.

Fisher, K., Geenen, J., Jurcevic, M. McClintock, K., Davis, G. (2009) 'Applying asset-based community development as a strategy for CSR: a Canadian perspective on a win–win for stakeholders and SMEs.' *Business Ethics: A European Review*, 18(1) pp. 66-82.

Freeman, R.E. (2010) *Strategic Management: A Stakeholder Approach.* Cambridge: Cambridge University Press.

Freeman, R.E. and Evan, W. (1990) 'Corporate governance: A stakeholder interpretation.' *The Journal of Behavioral Economics*, 19(4), pp. 337-359.

Freeman, R.E., Harrison, J. S., Wicks, A. C., Parmar, B. L., Colle, S. (2010) *Stakeholder Theory: The State of the Art.* Cambridge: Cambridge University Press.

Fuller, T. and Tian, Y. (2006) 'Social and Symbolic Capital and Responsible Entrepreneurship: An Empirical Investigation of SME Narratives.' *Journal of Business Ethics*, 67(3) pp. 287-304.

Garriga, E. and Melé, D. (2004) 'Corporate social responsibility theories: Mapping the territory.' *Journal of Business Ethics*, 53(1/2) pp. 51–71.

Gilde GmbH. (2007) *Commitment to society by small and medium-sized enterprises in Germany – Current situation and future development.* Detmold: Gilde GmbH. [Online] [Accessed on 21st April 2020] https://www.google.com/url?sa=t&rct=j&q=&esrc=s&source=web&cd=1&ved=2ahUKEwig7ealiProAhUME8AKHYGJBLYQFjAAegQIAhAB&url=http%3A%2F%2Fwww.csr-mittelstand.de%2Fpdf%2FStudie_CSR_im_Mittelstand_Deutschland_EN.pdf

Graves, S.B. and Waddock, S.A. (1994) 'Institutional Owners and Corporate Social Performance.' *Academy of Management Journal*, 37(4), pp. 1034-1046.

Gray, E.R. and Balmer, J.M.T. (1998) 'Managing corporate image and corporate reputation.' *Long Range Planning*, 31(5) pp. 695-702.

GRI. (2014) *Bereit für den Nachhaltigkeitsbericht? Nachhaltigkeitsbericht für KMU.* Amsterdam: GRI. [Online] [Accessed on 7th January 2021] https://docplayer.org/35454-Bereit-fuer-den-nachhaltigkeitsbericht.html

Habisch, A. (2004) 'Social Responsibility, Social Capital and SMEs.' *In* Spence, L.J., Habisch, A. and Schmidpeter R. (eds.) *Responsibility and Social Capital: The World of Small and Medium Sized Enterprises.* Basingstoke: Palgrave Macmillan, pp. 25-34.

Harrison, J.S., Bosse, D.A. and Phillips, R.A. (2010) 'Managing for stakeholders, stakeholder utility functions and competitive advantage.' *Strategic Management Journal*, 31(1) pp. 58-74.

Heblich, S. and Gold, R. (2008) *Corporate Social Responsibility. Eine win-win Strategie für Unternehmen und Regionen.* Jena: IHK für Niederbayern in Passau/Max-Planck Institut für Ökonomik. [Online] [Accessed on 21st April 2020] https://www.researchgate.net/publication/42241763_Corporate_Social_Responsibility_eine_win-win_Strategie_fur_Unternehmen_und_Regionen

Hendry, J. (2001) 'Missing the Target: Normative Stakeholder Theory and the Corporate Governance Debate.' *Business Ethics Quarterly* 11(1) pp. 159-176.

Humber, J.M. (2002) 'Beyond stockholders and stakeholders: A plea for corporate moral autonomy.' *Journal of Business Ethics*, 36(3) pp. 207-221.

Hungenberg, H. (2014) *Strategisches Management in Unternehmen: Ziele – Prozesse – Verfahren.* 8th ed., Wiesbaden: Gabler Verlag.

Icks, A., Levering, B., Maaß, F. and Werner, A. (2015) Chancen und Risiken von CSR im Mittelstand. Bonn: IfM [Online] [Accessed on 25th June 2020] https://www.ifm-bonn.org//uploads/tx_ifmstudies/IfM-Materialien-236_2015.pdf

IfM Bonn. (2020a) *Definitionen.* IfM Bonn. [Online] [Accessed on 7th April 2020] https://www.ifm-bonn.org/definitionen/

IfM Bonn. (2020b) *KMU-Definition der IfM Bonn.* IfM Bonn. [Online][Accessed on 7th April 2020] https://www.ifm-bonn.org/definitionen/kmu-definition-des-ifm-bonn/

IfM Bonn. (2020c) Frequently Asked Questions (FAQ). IfM Bonn. [Online] [Accessed on 25th June 2020] https://en.ifm-bonn.org/faq/#accordion=0&tab=1

IfM Bonn. (2020d) *Unternehmensbestand.* IfM Bonn. [Online] [Accessed on 7th April 2020] https://www.ifm-bonn.org/statistiken/unternehmensbestand/#accordion=0&tab=0

Jamali, D., Zanhour, M., Keshishian, T. (2009) 'Peculiar Strengths and Relational Attributes of SMEs in the Context of CSR.' Journal of Business Ethics, 87(3), pp. 355-377.

Jenkins, H. (2004) 'A Critique of Conventional CSR Theory: An SME Perspective.' *Journal of General Management*, 29(4), pp. 37-57.

Jenkins, H. (2006) 'Small and Medium-Sized Enterprises & Corporate Social Responsibility: Identifying the Knowledge Gaps.' *Journal of Business Ethics*, 67(3), pp. 241-256.

Jenkins, H. (2009) 'A ,business opportunity' model of corporate social responsibility for small-and medium-sized enterprises.' *Business Ethics: A European Review*, 18(1), pp. 21-36.

Jensen, M.C. (2002) 'Value Maximization, Stakeholder Theory, and the Corporate Objective Function.' *Business Ethics Quarterly* 12(2) pp. 235-256.

Jonker, J., Stark, W. and Tewes, S. (2011) *Corporate Social Responsibility und nachhaltige Entwicklung: Einführung, Strategie und Glossar*. Heidelberg: Gabler Springer.

Kechiche, A. and Soparnot, R. (2012) 'CSR within SMEs: Literature Review.' *International Business Research*, 5(7) pp. 97-104.

Kim, H.L., Rhou, Y., Uysal, M. and Kwon, N. (2017) 'An examination of the links between corporate social responsibility (CSR) and its internal consequences.' *International Journal of Hospitality Management*, 61 pp. 26-34.

Knudson, H. (2018) *Making the business case: The effects of corporate social responsibility on SME competitiveness*. Unknown place of publication: Interreg Europe [Online] [Accessed on 7th January 2021] https://www.interregeurope.eu/fileadmin/user_upload/tx_tevprojects/library/file_1523518061.pdf

Kranzusch, P., May-Strobl, E., Levering, B., Welter, F., Ettl, K. (2017) *Das Zukunftspanel Mittelstand 2017 – Update einer Expertenbefragung zu aktuellen und zukünftigen Herausforderungen des deutschen Mittelstands*. Bonn: IfM Bonn. [Online] [Accessed on 7th April 2020] https://www.ifm-bonn.org//uploads/tx_ifmstudies/IfM-Materialien-256_2017.pdf

Księżak, P. and Fischbach, B. (2017) 'Tripple Bottom Line: The Pillars of CSR.' *Journal of Corporate Responsibility and Leadership*, 4(3) pp. 96-110.

Lepoutre, J. and Heene, A. (2006) 'Investigating the Impact of Firm Size on Small Business Social Responsibility: A Critical Review.' *Journal of Business Ethics*, 67(3) pp. 257-273.

Lu, J., Ren, L., Zhang, C., Rong, D., Ahmed, R. R., Streimikis, J. (2020) 'Modified Carroll's pyramid of corporate social responsibility to enhance organizational performance of SMEs industry.' *Journal of Cleaner Production*, 271 pp. 1-18.

Lynch-Wood, G., Williamson, D., Jenkins, W. (2009) 'The over-reliance on self-regulation in CSR policy.' *Business Ethics*,18(1) pp. 52-65.

Maaß, F. and Clemens, R. (2002) *Corporate Citizenship: Das Unternehmen als 'guter Bürger'*. Wießbaden: Institut für Mittelstandsforschung (IfM). [Online] [Accessed on 21st April 2020] https://www.ifm-bonn.org// uploads/tx_ifmstudies/94_nf.pdf

Maaß, F. (2007) *CSR and Competitiveness European SMEs' Good Practice: National Report Germany*. Bonn: Institut für Mittelstandsforschung (IfM). [Online] [Accessed on 21st April 2020] https://www.ifm-bonn.org// uploads/tx_ifmstudies/CSR-Germany.pdf

Maaß, F. (2010) *Wirtschaftspolitische Ansätze zur Unterstützung von Corporate Social Responsibility-Aktivitäten*. Bonn: Institut für Mittelstandsforschung (IfM). [Online] [Accessed on 21st April 2020] https://www.ifm-bonn.org//uploads/tx_ifmstudies/IfM-Materialien-194_2010.pdf

Maaß, F., Chlosta, S., Icks, A., Welter, F. (2014) *Konzepte und Wirkungen nachhaltigen Unternehmertums*. Bonn: Institut für Mittelstandsforschung Bonn (IfM). [Online] [Accessed on 21st April 2020] https://www.ifm-bonn.org//uploads/tx_ifmstudies/IfM-Materialien-227.pdf

Maldonado-Erazo, C.P., Álvarez-García, J., de la Cruz del Río-Rama, M., Correa-Quezada, R. (2020) 'Corporate Social Responsibility and Performance in SMEs: Scientific Coverage.' *Sustainability*, 12(6) pp. 47-62.

Marcoux, A. M. (2000) 'Balancing Act.' *In* DesJardins, J. R. and McCall, J. J. (eds.) *Contemporary Issues in Business Ethics*. 4th ed., Wadsworth Publishing, pp. 92-100.

Margolis, D. J. and Walsh J. P. (2003) 'Misery Loves Companies: Rethinking Social Initiatives by Business.' *Administrative Science Quarterly*, 48(2) pp. 268-305.

McWilliams, A., Siegel, D.S, Wright, P.M. (2006) 'Corporate Social Responsibility: Strategic Implications.' *Journal of Management Studies*, 43(1), pp. 1-18.

Mellahi, K., Frynas, J. G., Sun, P., Siegel, D. (2016) 'A Review of the Nonmarket Strategy Literature: Toward a Multi-Theoretical Integration.' *Journal of Management*, 42(1) pp. 143-173.

Mitchell, R.K., Agle, B.R. and Wood, D.J. (1997) 'Toward a Theory of Stakeholder Identification and Salience: Defining the Principle of Who and What Really Counts.' *The Academy of Management Review*, 22(4) pp. 853-886.

Mitchell, R.K., Agle, B R., Chrisman, J.J. and Spence, L.J. (2011) 'Toward a Theory of Stakeholder Salience in Family Firms.' *Business Ethics Quarterly,* 21(2) pp. 235-255.

Mohnen, A. (2018) *Familienunternehmen als Arbeitgeber: Die Einstellungen und Erwartungen junger Fach- und Führungskräfte*. München: Stiftung Familienunternehmen. [Online] [Accessed on 25th June 2020] https://www.familienunternehmen.de/media/public/pdf/publikationen-studien/studien/Die-Einstellungen-und-Erwartungen-junger-Fach-und-Fuehrungskraefte_Studie_Stiftung-Familienunternehmen.pdf

Morsing, M. and Perrini, F. (2009) 'CSR in SMEs: do SMEs matter for the CSR agenda?' *Business Ethics: A European Review*, 18(1) pp. 1-6.

Murillo, D. and Lozano, J.M. (2006) 'SMEs and CSR: An Approach to CSR in their Own Words.' *Journal of Business Ethics*, 67(3) pp. 227-240.

Nahapiet, J. and Ghoshal, S. (1998) 'Social Capital, Intellectual Capital, and the Organizational Advantage.' *The Academy of Management Review*, 23(2) pp. 242-266.

OECD. (2009) *Human Capital: How what you know shapes your life*. Paris: OECD Publishing.

Orts, E. W. and Alan Strudler (2002) 'The Ethical and Environmental Limits of Stakeholder Theory.' *Business Ethics Quarterly,* 12(2) pp. 215-234.

Parker, C.M., Bellucci, E., Zutshi, A., Torlina, L. and Fraunholz, B. (2015) 'SME stakeholder relationship descriptions in website CSR communications.' *Social Responsibility Journal*, 11(2) pp. 364-386.

Parmar, B.L, Freeman, R.E, Harrison, J.S., Wicks, A.C., De Colle, S. and Rurnell, L. (2010) 'Stakeholder Theory: The State of the Art.' *The Academy of Management Annals*, 3(1), pp. 403-445.

Perrini, F. (2006) 'SMEs and CSR Theory: Evidence and Implications from an Italian Perspective.' *Journal of Business Ethics*, 67(3) pp. 305-316.

Perrini, F., Russo, A., Tencati, A. (2007) 'CSR strategies of SMEs and large firms. Evidence from Italy.' *Journal of Business Ethics,* 74(3), pp. 285-300.

Phillips, R., Freeman, R.E. and Wicks, A.C. (2003) 'What stakeholder theory is not.' *Business Ethics Quarterly,* 13(4), pp. 479-502.

Pivato, S., Misnai, N. and Tencati, A. (2008) 'The impact of corporate social responsibility on consumer trust: The case of organize food.' *Business Ethics: A European Review*, 17(1) pp. 3-12.

Porter, M.E. and Kramer, M.R. (2006) 'Strategy and society: The Link Between Competitive Advantage and Corporate Social Responsibility.' *Harvard Business Review*, December, pp. 1-13.

Post, J.E, Preston, L.E. and Sachs, S. (2002) 'Managing the extended enterprise: The new stakeholder view.' *California Management Review*, 45(1) pp. 6-28.

Pott, C., Axjonow, A., Weinland, M. (2017) *Nachhaltigkeit im Mittelstand: Corporate Social Responsibility (CSR): Strategien, Organisation und Berichtswesen*. Unknown place of publication: Bakertilly. [Online] [Accessed on 7th April 2020] https://www.bakertilly.de/aktuelles/publikationen/detailansicht/corporate-social-responsibility-csr-studie-nachhaltigkeit-im-mittelstand.html

Preuss, L. and Perschke, J. (2010) 'Slipstreaming the Larger Boats: Social Responsibility in Medium-Sized Businesses.' *Journal of Business Ethics*, 92(4) pp. 531-551.

Puncheva, P. (2008) 'The role of corporate reputation in the stakeholder decision-making process.' *Business & Society*, 47(3) pp. 272-290.

Putnam, R. D. (1995) 'Tuning In, Tuning Out: The Strange Disappearance of Social Capital in America.' *PS: Political Science & Politics*, 28(4) pp. 664-683.

Rawls, J. (1993) *Political Liberalism*. New York: Columbia University Press.

Roberts, S., Lawson, R., Nicholls, J. (2006) 'Generating Regional-Scale Improvements in SME Corporate Responsibility Performance: Lessons from Responsibility Northwest.' *Journal of Business Ethics*, 67(3) pp. 275-286.

Russo, A., Tencati, A. (2009) 'Formal Vs informal CSR strategies: evidence from Italian micro, small, medium-sized and large firms.' *Journal of Business Ethics*, 85(S2) pp. 339-353.

Russo, A. and Perrini, F. (2010) 'Investigating Stakeholder Theory and Social Capital: CSR in Large Firms and SMEs.' *Journal of Business Ethics*, 91(2) pp. 207-221.

Sachs, S. and Rühli, E. (2005) 'Changing Managers' Values towards a Broader Stakeholder Orientation.' *Corporate Governance: International Journal for Business in Society*, 5(2) pp. 89-98.

Saunders, M. and Lewis, P. (2012) *Doing Research in Business & Management: An Essential Guide to Planning Your Project*. Essex: Pearson.

Saunders, M.N.K., Lewis, P. and Thornhill, A. (2019) *Research methods for business students*. 8th ed. New York: Pearson.

Scrivens, K. and Smith, C. (2013) *Four Interpretations of Social Capital: An Agenda for Measurement*. OECD Statistics Working Papers 2013/06, Working Paper No 55. [Online] [Accessed on 7th June 2021] https://doi.org/10.1787/5jzbcx010wmt-en

Sen, S. and Bhattacharya, C.B. (2001) 'Does Doing Good Always Lead to Doing Better? Consumer Reactions to Corporate Social Responsibility.' *Journal of Marketing Research*, 38(2) pp. 225-243.

Smith, N.C. (2003) 'Corporate social responsibility: Whether or how?' *California Management Review*, 45(4) pp. 52-76.

Spence, L.J. (1999) 'Does size matter? The state of the art in small business ethics.' *Business Ethics: A European Review*, 8(3) pp. 163-174.

Spence, L.J. and Lozano, J.F. (2000) 'Communicating about ethics with small firms: experiences from the UK and Spain.' *Journal of Business Ethics* 27(1/2) pp. 43-53.

Spence, L.J. and Rutherfoord, R. (2001) 'Social responsibility, profit maximisation and the small firm owner-manager.' *Journal of Small Business and Enterprise Development*, 8(2) pp. 126-139.

Spence, L.J., Schmidtpeter, R., and Habisch, A. (2003) 'Assessing Social Capital: Small and Medium Sized Enterprises in Germany and the U.K.' *Journal of Business Ethics*, 47(1) pp. 17-29.

Spence, L.J., Rutherfoord, R. (2003) 'Small Business and Empirical Perspectives in Business Ethics: Editorial.' *Journal of Business Ethics*, 47(1) pp. 1-5.

Taneja, S., Taneja, P., Gupta, R. (2011) 'Researches in CSR: a review of shifting focus, paradigms and methodologies.' *Journal of Business Ethics*, 101(3) pp. 343-364.

UN. (2020) *Sustainable Development Goals*. Unknown place of publication: UN. [Online] [Accessed on 7th January 2021] https://www.un.org/sustainabledevelopment/wp-content/uploads/2019/01/SDG_Guidelines_AUG_2019_Final.pdf

UN Global Compact. (2020) *The Ten Pinciples of the UN Global Compact.* [Online] [Accessed on 7th January 2021] https://www.unglobalcompact.org/what-is-gc/mission/principles

Vázquez-Carrasco, R. and López-Pérez, M.E. (2013) 'Small & medium-sized enterprises and corporate social responsibility: A systematic review of the literature.' *Qual Quant*, 47(6) pp. 3205–3218.

Von Weltzien, H. and Shankar, D. (2011) 'How can SMEs in a cluster respond to global demands for CSR.' *Journal of Business Ethics*, 101(2) pp. 175-195.

Wang, H., Tong, L., Takeuchi, R. and George, G. (2016) 'Corporate Social Responsibility: An Overview And New Research Directions.' *Academy of Management Journal*, 59(2) pp. 534-544.

Waddock, S. (2004) 'Parallel universes: Companies, Academics, and the Progress of Corporate Citizenship.' *Business and Society Review*, 109(1) pp. 5-42.

Waddock, S., Bodwell, C. and Graves, S. B. (2002) 'Responsibility: The new business imperative.' *Academy of Management Perspectives*, 16(2) pp. 132-148.

Weber, M. (2008) 'The business case for corporate social responsibility: A company-level measurement approach for CSR.' *European Management Journal*, 26(4), pp. 247-261.

Weiß, M. (2005) 'Which social responsibility for the enterprise? The German case.' *Managerial Law,* 47(5) pp. 47-70.

Welge, M. Al-Laham, M., and Eulerich, M. (2017) *Strategisches Management: Grundlagen - Prozess - Implementierung.* 7th ed. Wiesbaden: Gabler Verlag.

Williamson, D., Lynch-Wood, G., and Ramsay, J. (2006) 'Drivers of environmental behavior in manufacturing SMEs and the implications for CSR.' *Journal of Business Ethics*, 67(3) pp. 317-330.

Appendices

Appendix 1 – Data

Note: 2007 A = Gilde GmbH 2007 B = Bertelsmann			Data Note: 1 = 100%			
Key factor	**Nr.**	**Sub-aspects**	2007 A	2007 B	2012	2017
Awareness	1.	Very Important	0.270	/	0.319	0.340
	2.	Important	0.400	/	0.475	0.450
	3.	Less Important	0.240	/	0.180	0.150
	4.	Not Important	0.090	/	0.026	0.050
Motiva-tion/Goals	5.	Improvement of Reputation	0.860	0.640	0.690	0.690
	6.	Motivation of Employees	0.720	0.800	0.770	0.700
	7.	Increase of Economic Success	0.570	0.410	0.648	0.620
	8.	Meeting Customers' Expectations	0.470	0.570	0.800	0.520
	9.	Cost Reduction	0.420	0.380	0.650	0.600
	10.	Ethical Motivation	0.430	0.820	/	0.580
	11.	Environmental Motivation	/	0.600	/	0.590
	12.	Securing Future Existence of Firm	/	0.450	0.798	0.840
Challenges	13.	Lack of Financial Resources	0.540	0.720	/	0.210
	14.	Lack of Human Resources	0.650	0.500	/	0.420
	15.	Insufficient Knowledge of CSR	0.620	0.320	/	0.280
	16.	Lack of Interest from Stake-holders	0.350	0.290	/	0.440
	17.	Doubts concerning the Usefulness of CSR	0.220	0.330	/	0.370
	18.	Lack of Time	0.650	0.750	/	0.550
	19.	Rules and Policies	/	0.550	/	0.210
Activities						
	20.	Continuous Training	0.860	0.940	0.755	0.930

Commitment to Employees	21.	Personalised Organisation of Working Hours	0.830	/	0.745	0.920
	22.	Compatibility of Work and Family	0.440	0.560	0.745	0.850
	23.	Additional Social Services and Securities	0.610	0.610	0.705	0.670
	24.	Promotion of Health and Safety	0.550	0.340	0.600	0.810
Commitment to Society	25.	Promotion and Support of Social Initiatives	0.710	0.720	0.560	0.840
	26.	Promotion and Support of Training Initiatives	0.690	0.390	0.560	0.660
	27.	Promotion and Support of Cultural Initiatives	0.550	0.560	0.560	0.610
	28.	Promotion and Support of Sport Initiatives	0.590	0.720	0.560	0.680
	29.	Principles of Anti-Corruption	0.510	/	0.530	0.520
Commitment to Environment	30.	Reduction of Energy Consumption	0.760	0.830	0.740	0.900
	31.	Measures for Sustainable Resource Use	0.690	0.770	0.650	0.840
	32.	Recycling	0.640	0.790	0.735	0.760
	33.	Environmentally Friendly Production Process	0.500	/	0.598	0.480
	34.	Reduction of Emission	0.480	0.566	0.625	0.600
	35.	Ecological Standard in Supply Chain	0.420	0.580	0.440	0.340
	36.	Use of Renewable Energy	0.340	/	0.595	0.540
Communication	37.	Website and Internet	0.320	0.190	0.680	0.680
	38.	Reports	0.060	0.380	0.570	0.330
	39.	Marketing campaigns and Press	0.120	0.430	0.610	0.390
	40.	Events and Internal Information	0.240	0.230	0.680	0.680

Appendix 2 – Index Numbers and Percentage Change Analysis

Analysis: Index Numbers							Analysis: Percentage Change in %			
Note: small and medium-sized firm (SMF); large-sized firm (LF)										
	SMF			LF			SMF		LF	
Nr.	2007 A	2012	2017	2007 B	2012	2017	2012	2017	2012	2017
1.	100	118	126	/	/	/	18	26	/	/
2.	100	119	113	/	/	/	19	13	/	/
3.	100	75	63	/	/	/	-25	-38	/	/
4.	100	29	56	/	/	/	-71	-44	/	/
5.	100	80	80	100	108	108	-20	-20	8	8
6.	100	107	97	100	96	88	7	-3	-4	-13
7.	100	114	109	100	158	151	14	9	58	51
8.	100	170	111	100	140	91	70	11	40	-9
9.	100	155	143	100	171	158	55	43	71	58
10.	100	/	135	100	/	71	/	35	/	-29
11.	/	/	/	100	/	98	/	/	/	-2
12.	/	/	/	100	177	187	/	/	77	87
13.	100	/	39	100	/	29	/	-61	/	-71
14.	100	/	65	100	/	84	/	-35	/	-16
15.	100	/	45	100	/	88	/	-55	/	-13
16.	100	/	126	100	/	152	/	26	/	52
17.	100	/	168	100	/	112	/	68	/	12
18.	100	/	85	100	/	73	/	-15	/	-27
19.	/	/	/	100	/	38	/	/	/	-62
20.	100	88	108	100	80	99	-12	8	-20	-1
21.	100	90	111	/	/	/	-10	11	/	/
22.	100	169	193	100	133	152	69	93	33	52

23.	100	116	110	100	116	110	16	10	16	10
24.	100	109	147	100	176	238	9	47	76	138
25.	100	79	118	100	78	117	-21	18	-22	17
26.	100	81	96	100	144	169	-19	-4	44	69
27.	100	102	111	100	100	109	2	11	0	9
28.	100	95	115	100	78	94	-5	15	-22	-6
29.	100	104	102	/	/	/	4	2	/	/
30.	100	97	118	100	89	108	-3	18	-11	8
31.	100	94	122	100	84	109	-6	22	-16	9
32.	100	115	119	100	93	96	15	19	-7	-4
33.	100	120	96	/	/	/	20	-4	/	/
34.	100	130	125	100	110	106	30	25	10	6
35.	100	105	81	100	76	59	5	-19	-24	-41
36.	100	175	159	/	/	/	75	59	/	/
37.	100	213	213	100	358	358	113	113	258	258
38.	100	950	550	100	150	87	850	450	50	-13
39.	100	508	325	100	142	91	408	225	42	-9
40.	100	283	283	100	296	296	183	183	196	196

Zeitfracht Medien GmbH
Ferdinand-Jühlke-Straße 7
99095 Erfurt, Deutschland
produktsicherheit@kolibri360.de